*The Bridge Between Matter & Spirit*
*is*
MATTER BECOMING SPIRIT

*The Bridge Between Matter & Spirit is*

*MATTER*
*BECOMING*
*SPIRIT*

THE ARCOLOGY OF PAOLO SOLERI

ANCHOR BOOKS
ANCHOR PRESS/DOUBLEDAY
*Garden City, New York*
1973

Anchor Books Edition
ISBN: 0-385-02361-8
Library of Congress Catalog Card Number 72–87501

Grateful acknowledgment is made to the following sources for
permission to use the following article, which appears in this
volume in adapted form:
"Utopia" which appeared in the Spring 1972 issue of *Journal
of California Tomorrow* Vol. 7 No. 2 copyright © 1972 by
Paolo Soleri; reprinted by permission.

# CONTENTS

congruently developing. From this and only
from this can we hope to put equity into
the affairs of mankind.

I attempt to discriminate between beauty
as appearance and beauty
as substance maintaining that the true
esthetic process is where man as a person
and man as "entelechy" of life combine
and become participant in the creation of a
compassionate universe. The creative act is
universal because it is highly personal.

*Topics* refer to some of what I consider the
most comprehensive aspects of the
planetary urbanization. This process is
overtly defined as a cosmic phenomenon
submitted to the laws of mass-energy and
working according to the methodology life
has been developing from its inception. The
methodological instrument for the
transformation of matter into spirit.
The questions are converging into the
overriding reservation about arcology. The
fear of depersonalization. The true origin
and cause of this fear is presently the
physical, economical, social and cultural
state of contemporary man. If what is
advocated here is admittedly so different
from such state, and if it stems from the
structure of evolution itself, it is at least
reasonable to suspect as a consequence the
opposite of depersonalization.

As the means seem to become more and more the master of the ends, life and man within it, I attempt here to keep open the well proven and operational case of the transrational, the spirit. Its development is dependent on new forms in which old and new functions find, a posteriori, favorable receptacles. This sequence is not unlike the "form" of the solar system and the earth becoming the receptacle of the function of life and translife.

Who is paid homage to in this paper is not really the craftsman but the artisan, the person capable of transforming routine, the bulk of life, into grace. This ability is often if not always beyond contemporary Western man. Nor has Western man found a substitute, if one exists, for such transformation and such fulfillment. This routine remains as it is, an integral part of our lives (automatism), but the ritual of it has withered away.

Flying over Europe is to eyewitness the massiveness of man's imprint on the earth. Forests and prairies have given way to farming and urbanization. Europe is a metaphysical stage of her former self. Is the evolution now reversing itself?

processes. The cleaning up of those
processes will often mean an even greater
pollution of life. I call the result a better
quality of wrongness, a further step toward
the coercion and punishment of the spirit.

The effacement of an instrument is sure sign
of an evolutionary step. The less intrusive
our instrumental world is (and logistics
are a good percentage of it), the smaller its
size, and the least energy hungry, the more
the mind of man will be capable of taking
itself with the body into the beyond of
matter. This will come about only if
concurrently the complexity of life is
winding itself up.

The simplistic contention that well-planned
mass transportation will do the job of
desegregating people, performances, and
environments by the miracle of speed is
getting to be too stale and costly. Our
operational grids, the city layouts, are
abstractions, and nothing will do in solving
the logistics of life. We had better look at
the greater master of all, the biological
methodology. There and only there lies the
answer.

The more power we hold the more in
ourselves is the potential for good and evil.
Unless we are able to guide ourselves by

the light we must see far out there in the
future, a light eons in the making, we will
be forever mired in futile battles. The
battle, for instance, for producing more
and better wrong things.

A sure way of doing harm to man is to let
one side of him-her wither away.
Psychosomatic man must be kept informed
not only by way of abstracts but roundly.
The body and the brain make up the
person. The senses, all the senses, must be
advised well as they are the windows to
knowledge and wisdom.

It is difficult to distinguish in the
contemporary American scene what is
withdrawal from what is rout; the future
will tell. In either case we are at best
making our future by default and we
cannot go on this way for long, as the
dulling of the soul is aquiescence toward
non-life.

Written in quasi-total ignorance of the
Freudian world, this might well be the
most naïve of all the papers. It could be
taken as an example of environmental
information (experienced) not
corroborated by remote (read, etc.)
information, thus lacking roundness, and
yet . . .

We are not genetically "finalized," as that
would imply a divorce from the
environmental influences whose forces are
still and "forever" powerfully working on
the manifestations of life, man included.

*As man is a responsible constructor of the environment he is unavoidably influencing his own genetic structure.*

PAUL VALÉRY    VARIÉTÉ IV

"Le présent nous apparaît comme une conjoncture sans précédent et sans exemple, un conflit sans issue entre des *choses qui ne savent pas mourir* et des *choses qui ne peuvent pas vivre.*"


"On peut dire que l'homme, s'éloignant de plus en plus, et bien plus rapidement que jamais, de ses conditions primitives d'existence, il arrive que *tout ce qu'il sait,* c'est-à-dire *tout ce qu'il peut, s'oppose* fortement à ce *qu'il est.*"

*For the spirit to be born and to become, matter and energy have to be manipulated. Capturings and manipulations have to be highly selective and demanding. Flesh is the transfigured matter made into a new kind of energy, the living energy that winds itself up by consuming.*

# PREFACE

We, the contemporary (Western) family of man, seem to hold the unique and unprecedented position of a living disaster. By a chorus of knowledgeable consent, we are not only obstructing the construction of a better world, we are close to bringing life to a crashing halt.

It would be pretty ironic if, as we come close to the artificial threshold of the third millennium, we would by data and superstition, by hunches and "hard facts," by corruption of ideas, heart and deeds, by failure of the will, find ourselves psychologically and mass-hysterically ready for the millennium and the nemesis of the gods. It would be ironic because our conceited view has been that, for all our faults, superstition and terminal bigotry were not our bag. With the age of enlightment between us and the dark ages, with renaissance, science, rationalization, technology, democracy, marxism, socialism, technocracy, moon shots, microbiology, etc., with the power of the mind wrapped around the power of the bulldozer, with the blossoming of materialism-opulence, we had left the gloom

and the anguish behind, the demons of the apocalypse
in the desert and the dust of ignorance. . . .

I do not bow to the death wish we exhibit cynically as a
sign of existential responsibility, nor do I sympathize with
the pietists sporting the flowing robes, beards and sandals
of the simple and the meek. I find the hard-headed
technocrat utterly pulp-minded; and the politician, too
busy to know and to be serious, I find him smothering the
soul, while flushing history into the past as if it were an
undigestible but somehow homogeneable slut.

I see most of the equivocation, the inability to connect,
synthesize, communicate, act, as the gap between the
nuts and bolts fanatic and the spiritualist not to mention
the "mystic," the inspired, the possessed. The chasm
seems unbridgeable and the pontoons floating on the
metaphoric and not so metaphoric blood of the species,
all the species, seem only to carry fragments of knowledge
too small for recognition. The dialogue is then more of an
artillery exchange only broadcasting destruction and
hardly any reception other than barrages and blows from
the other side. Yet both the matter-of-factness man and the
metaphysician are there because the adversary is there
also. The bridge above the chasm and the shamble is
ultimately the marvel of subtlety into which "mass energy"
is able to convert itself, and both men are the builders of
it.

The bridge between matter and spirit is *matter becoming spirit*. This flow from the indefinite-infinite into the
utterly subtle is the moving arch pouring physical matter
into the godliness of conscious and metaphysical energy.
This is the context, the place where we must begin anew.

There are not really two shores and the chasm of ir-
reconciliation in between, but there is an anchorage, the
physical mooring and a radiance emanating from it. The
physical mooring is "locally established" at every instance
of action. The radiance is the glow emitted whenever the

metamorphosis of matter into spirit has begun. This radiance begins only in those instances where the organized matter becomes ultra-organized into a transcendence of itself, a future generator, a creating trans-machine. Technology is neither the mooring nor the radiance. It is a media useful in the actual transformation. It is matter manipulated into equipment for growth. When such equipment becomes the message then there is no message, technological sophistication perhaps, but not a thing to do with it. The opposite of this functional emptiness is the concept of God, the pure spirit for whom the media has been obliterated and only the message-spirit remains. And this is not because the whole extant reality has become the media, therefore the message, but because the intensity of the message has metamorphosized the media into part of the message. For lack of such (divine) intensity, the media and the message are apart only to coincide again at the entropic end (the end opposite to the spirit) where the message is zero and the media is an endless wasteland.

Then technology is not all there is (Fuller). It is what there is that we can use to create a transtechnological universe. The "we" is itself technology in every instance where the (existential) norm is maintentive, the housekeeping of a cosmos which true reality is in its own transformation in a better self. For a cosmos whose "what" is technology, the "why" does not matter as there is no focality nor good and evil in it. For a cosmos whose "what" is the spirit, the "why" is creation and the "how" is technology.

What is such technology? It is the constructing skill making the bridge. The bridge, this singular train of structures, founded on mineral moorings and perpetually surging away from them, saturating itself of spirit as it is, is still, and mandatorily so, made of mineral stuff more or less subtly manipulated and refined by life and man. Not only tissues and flesh out of "soil and sun," but also steel out of ore, plastics out of oil, etc. The physical structure is still the skeleton of the spirit, and structure is the bridge-train on which the spirit travels and grows stronger. The physical energy consumed in the durational journey goes ultimately into the generation of the life energy which, as knowledge, is not constrained by the physical law of energy conservation but transcends it by creating out of itself more of itself. We call this creation of mental energy the "learning process," the incrementation of knowledge, the process of civilization.

The technological methodology ever present when this process is active is threeheaded: complexity, miniaturization and their durational deployment. This is the trinity which makes the stone glow and become spirit. In their absence even God becomes a weak, tenuous, simplistic hypothesis. How far we are from the condition where the message has dissolved the media, the theoretical godhead, is apparent if we look at the present extrabiological technology. We find it to be the great oversimplifier. Technology, as we have it now, is the resolver of one-at-a-time aspects of a problem that, is always far more faceted and outreaching than any of each of its aspects. Technology focuses on one of the corners and single-mindedly forces a solution, the local solution. Often, if not always, there isn't such a thing as often-if-not-always and for the same reason practical man fails real man. If there is any comprehensive definition of pollution it has to be found in the failure of technology to account for a true tuning in on a problem in its totality. That is to say, its failure in fostering the spirit. If the reference "point" is the spirit then whenever spirit is not incremented, pollution is present in its most comprehensive form: entropy. Entropy and pollution are one and the same.

This group of papers spanning about ten years are related to one another through the conviction that as there is more to man than economics, politics, survival and the pursuit of happiness, there better be more in the physical environment than what man (Western man and non-Western man) is bent on doing now. That the unbroken spiral that has brought spirit out of stone is still climbing upward and the instrumentality he needs in this miraculous pursuit must be up to the task.

An apology if so much of the writing sounds like sermonizing and rambling about. The sermons are directed to myself and I am the first (the only?) in line trying to see if the written words are more than an idle exercise.

*Cosanti, Arizona*
*July 1972*

# THE BEAUTIFUL BODY IS AN AWESOME POWERHOUSE

Our technologists, our energy experts, our environmentalists, our social engineers, our politicians, our planners, our know-what and know-how men are faltering, stumbling, falling on their faces. I have come to the incredible conclusion that what seems to be obvious is totally unsuspected by the analyst-experts. Am I the only one who sees the direct, unbreakable constant, ineffable relationship (coincidence) between the "quality of life," and the complexity of its structure? To listen to any of them one cannot feel optimistic. Just the hope that they not be entrusted with the future of man. What is missing in their "scenarios" is not the depth of analytical intelligence but the insight on the real consequences of the cumulative victories the phenomenon of life has had, standing on and above the sound foundation of statistics and probability.

## LIFE VERSUS NON-LIFE

Those victories were and are all predicated on the ability of the living phenomenon to withstand the pressure of the non-living environment. Not for any devilish scheme carried on by this last, but for the simple if fundamental reason that non-life is the normal, universal condition of the extant cosmos. It does not take great scientific, philosophical or religious insight to understand that, of all hardships life is engaged in, this battle for survival is at the center of the stage. In fact, there is where the staging of life's journey begins, harnessed by electromagnetic-gravitational bridles on the threshold of ever-new experiences, tribulations, exhilarations, knowledge, creations. These physical harnesses are utterly indispensable as they are utterly unforgiving. They are the concreteness of life and the ballast that impedes its flight. The dialectic of the spiritual phenomenon is that total spirituality demands the impounding of the whole physical universe into the most comprehensive, encompassing "machine for creation." Then the crazy-quilt, patch-it-before-it-tears, grand designs of our intellectual elite is a dumb, dim, fallacious, hypocritical, fraudulent game smudged on the body of the real. The pietism of the hurried environmentalist clashes head on with the steel compassion inherent to the performance of the whole biosphere.

Telescoping on the brick, the wall goes out of focus making ecology an instant take-out of a process of eons. Life is frozen in and by a mental ice age. If, awed by the beauty of the patient and charitably upset by the break of grace perpetrated by a sizable scar, we were to refrain from a local surgery to find soon after that the illness has flared up in many new places, we would be doing in a medical context what we preach now in the environmental "game." We do not really contest the well-doing of a country opening up new candidacy on waste and squalor everywhere. That is progress and the pursuit of happiness. We simply, candidly and "objectively" insist that such scatterization from city nodules be well-planned; the well-planned cancer on the body of civilization and earth.

But things are far worse than that. Something is missing within the analogy. The patient is not it, he, her or them. The beautiful patient is us, the phenomenon of life. From concealed sadism the process moves, overt or not, to masochism . . . death wish? We act as if we were not able to brush away from the beautiful flesh of our body the germs that will then infect the skin and penetrate the flesh to burn the body and extinguish the soul. Not only do we seem not to have a future willed and pursued, but we court ever-new ills and epidemics by not observing the elementary rules of hygiene. Let one's own body do its own thing truly environmentally, sensorially, sensitively (beware of appearances). Do not let the crusts of insensitivity and segregation isolate and estrange one area or one organ from the next. Do not let the infection run unchecked. No, we just say that the infection is the sign of our healthy state, the growing pains of an undisciplined giant.

## THE CLUMSY GIANT

The giant is absurdly tearing itself apart, escaping from the self into the non-self, into the naught of a mental abstraction, called nature, that barrel of illusions, melancholy and obscurantism, that portrait by a mad painter or by a weekend poet at loss for things to do, that fantasy of the "outdoorsman," that mind-fabricated enchantress. Nature is far more and far beyond such fabrications. It is the myriads of furnaces of the stars. It is billions of tons of granite and iron. It is a quasi-infinity of mass-energy. It is time unraveling processes indefinitely. "Closer to us" nature is still immensely shattering the dusty corners of the mind. It is the monstrous manipulator of energy, the furnace of the sun's energy edging away with the sun's inexplicable action, from its own fury, to become the accumulator of thousands of cubic miles of ferns and forests, diatom and flesh, made into fossils, to become the unexhausted trigger of generation after generation of sensitive, sentient creatures, green and brown, black and white, diaphanous and opaque, quivering, "still," floating, crawling, running, flying, coming to life, processing and transforming, making the I and the Thou out of the it, etherealizing dirt and stone, making vagrant and gentle duration out of time, passing on and away . . . a transencyclopedia, living and portraying its own written words, the logos. A reality unfolding history, endlessly metamorphosizing its pragmatic self, a nature that neither the buck-hungry developer nor the starry-eyed (what stars?) youth, nor the self-righteous ecologist, nor any of the honest or not so honest band-wagoners is willing or able to see, and even less to take into account. In a way, the wildcat driller, the mine-stripper, the industrial tycoon or his domesticated counterpart are, recklessly no doubt, joining in a defiance of "nature" that suits better the demonism of both life and *Homo sapiens* in it. The thrust of life is more impetuous in them than it is in the piousness of the ecologist and his sacred status quo. Which is where the analogy is again falling short of the objective.

What is not accounted for is the durational transformism of reality as we live it on this earth. The "ourself," who is the subject, is not an event, perpetually reforming itself identically, but instead a self-creating "organism." Thus, the health care per se is tantamount to a desperate life condition bogged down to the drudgery of maintenance and a solipsistic narcissism with no trace of joy.

## LIFE'S CHAIN

The maintenance of the beautiful body is for the purpose of creating an ever more beautiful one, as the present one is nothing less or more than the fruitful "product" of a lesser beautiful body parent to it. It would not have come about without the trust and "knowledge" of the parents, themselves, another link in the chain of the self-making powerhouse of the real. If we ourselves pretend legitimacy (not to demand suicide) then automatically such right has, as a mirror image of itself, the imperative of creative continuity. A faulty link or a non-formed one is by far the least compassionate deed life can collapse into. A sin by default probably, a sin conjured by both lack of hope and lack of "vision."

## FROM MATTER TO SPIRIT

Thus, the beautiful body of the analogy is not only not skin cleansed and when necessary surgically freed from troublesome and menacing spots of infection, not only treated as if it really were not of our concern what the consequences might be, ignoring that it is our terrestrial and whole reality, but it is also, and especially by those who should know better, taken for what it is now and not for what it is becoming. A becoming which is long and uninterrupted, conservatively speaking, from the time when the sun cometh about in the skies. Why such becoming should be stopped cold now because fear or pietism order so has not been explained, as it has not been explained by another faction why the economic incentive must be the arbiter and ruler in its becoming.

What is the guiding thread that makes our intervention on the beautiful body right and legitimate? The one that most forcefully has for its outcome the transubstantiation of mass-energy into spirit. To reject or ignore this at this time and age is to be pretty blind and quite remote from the facts of the evolutionary transformation-transfiguration of an earth made from stone and fire into what it is now, a sensitized, sensitive, sentient, to say the very least, "spaceship" (space spirit) earth.

The same guidelines and methods this creature has invented to develop itself are here for us to adopt if we are really what we pretend to be, mind-endowed animals. We (I mean life on earth) can produce and organize one billion of billions of cells into a coral reef, and/or ultra-organize a comparable number of cells into a person. Side by side those two phenomena teach us a pretty solid lesson. There where the organization is more stringent, the inventions more subtle, the variety of events greater, the number of relationships more numerous, the sensitivity more developed, the responses less predictable, etc., that is to say there where the complexity is greater (millions of times greater in this instance), there is where the spirit is and prevails stronger. There is where is acted, and more impatiently, the whole drama of the massive, powerful thrust of what originally had been a torpid and brutish non-acquiescence to pure physicality-predictability and what is blossoming into the complex (and consequently) into the unpredictability of ever-increasing consciousness-knowledge, creativity.

As "cells" of unfathomably greater richness than the little innocent coral polypus, as it is granted and it is rejoiced, we, the quasi three billions of persons, are consciously and unconsciously working at the invention-conception of an ultra-person or trans-person who will place the family of today's man (in relative terms) in similar position as the coral reef colony, one overextended organism, stays to the organism of a mammal. (It has to be pointed out that I am simply referring here to the direct relationship between liveliness-spirit and complexity miniaturization, and not implying biological-morphological-ontological-theological compatibilities. Though on this score we must be more aware that classification and specified destinies are good working tools, not God-established categories.)

## RESPONSIBILITY

To say that the little polypus will go to enrich the lime of the ocean floor while a person will have to go to heaven or hell is just another way of saying that homo faber's responsibilities are myriads of times heavier than those of the coral fabricator are. The measure of the difference is written in the balance sheet of joy and sorrow, consciousness, compassion of both.

Where does miniaturization come in? It comes with complexity as the two are but two aspects of one phenomenon: the generation of consciousness within brute matter. The conceivability of a future whose complexity-liveliness stands to the present as the present degree of complexity-liveliness stands to the universe of the coral consciousness is only affordable by a phenomenology able to pack more and more of its own fire into lesser and lesser spaces. See the bio-technology of the brain as the most vivid example. See the electro-technology of the computer as a gross approximation of an extra-biological technology in store for the future. There is where the mindlessness of our planners becomes clear. Business as usual, or as usual with glamour, is not business at all. It is plain obscurantism. All the problems of population, of energy-demand (not energy need, by the way), of conservation of land, water, air, resources, species, etc., of waste and wastes, of pollution, of segregation, of frustration, of bureaucratic gigantism, of poverty, of pauperism, all but all of them are directly, indissolubly bound to the resourcefulness of our minds in dealing directly and forcefully with the coincidence if not identity between the quality of life, its complexity and the miniaturized character necessary for its containers.

The inability to identify this correlation that only consents the transfiguration of physics into metaphysic, that is to say, from the reality of four or so billions of years ago to the reality of today, this atonement guided by the crisis of yesterday, this head-in-the-sand of the defeathered biped, is what paralyzes our policies and pre-empts our plans. We act congruously with the thrust of life eons old or we put ourselves out of it altogether.

## U.S.A. BICENTENNIAL 1976

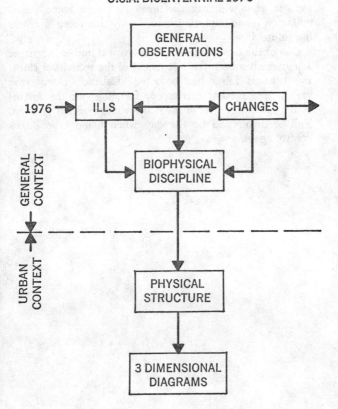

There is no compassion in a society pursuing some equity, when this same society defies the far more comprehensive equity of a self-creating reality. I dare anyone to dismiss the imperative of such congruence and still pretend to be responsible for his own acts. I dare anyone to say that as a "practitioner" he or she cannot dwell in metaphysics. I dare the technologist to maintain that hardware is what will make or break it. I dare homo faber, tailing on homo opportunisticus, to say that there is where the future is.

One of the homo faber's inventions was and is language. Language has been the instrument of the spirit ever since. By it homo faber has become "idealistic" (*logos*, the verb). Homo faber carries on, ferreting out the instruments for the genesis of ideas by which creation goes on. Full of dread will be the day when homo faber takes control again.

# A VIEW OF THE UNITED STATES—LOOKING TOWARD THE BICENTENNIAL 1976

## GENERAL OBSERVATIONS

Considering the bicentennial occasion as a pivot point from which to take stock of a past of graying nuances and of a future one seeks brighter, it is easier and possibly of some use to be epigrammatic and, quite possibly, dogmatic.

There is less and less reason to assume that the human race is purely an aggregate of individual phenomena forced to a promiscuous existence by the limited envelope of the earth. A mental sphere is gradually thickening and ribbing itself around the biosphere. The liveliness of this noosphere, as Teilhard de Chardin calls it, is the conscious and unconscious concern of mankind.

Since to assess the condition of man and look beyond the present is and will always be done from specific positions defined by the background of the writer, I am trying to see what physically can be given to the noosphere in terms of environment and instrumentality. This is a priority of first magnitude if we keep in mind that, once deprived of the universe of artifacts he has invented, man is the most naked and helpless of beings. We are, if anything, three things: we are environmental, we are social and we are cultural. That is to say, man is irrelevant when put out of the environmental, the social and the cultural context.

Coming down to "Homo Americanus," one might say that no continent can afford a one-voice representation as has the North American continent. Few exceptions aside, this one-voice representation is of the most fraudulent nature, clearly a fraudulence of substance not of representation. However will the destiny of the American nation and Canada conclude itself, the harshness and crudity of its continental (ecological) performance will be inscribed in history and will explain a lot of why its destiny got so warped.

Reared as much as it was on self-righteousness, bent as much as it was on a territorialism and an ownership often asserted above and against human rights and life, making a glorious saga of the Indian genocide, and a minor blemish of sanctioned and unsanctioned slavery, the American civilization has also made a point of pride to rape its own continent (adding ever-new dimensions to its destruction). We will not know what to do with ourselves, let alone celebrate a bicentennial, if we do not face the massive power for squalor we are exercising. We have made progress in our concern, if not in our practice, for those things that demand social equity; but we do not find interest in the problem of coherence between us and the geophysico-biological reality whose spherical envelope we are part and parcel of. This state of congruence is a pervasive necessity, embracing and containing the problem of equity itself. Equity is not possible outside the larger container of congruence. Congruence is really a condition of equity that has brought into its frame all the components that are usually ignored in the orthodoxy of social equity.

In the United States, granted overlappings and bivalences, one can see which ills are of inequity, which of incongruence. Racism, bigotry, greed, hypocrisy, intolerance and fear are working against equity. Unbalance between analytical work and synthetic trust, indifference toward the worsening environmental puzzle, unlimited permissiveness construed as freedom are working against congruence. A state of (apparent) social equity can thus be highly inequitable when observed from a position of congruence. This does not come from the subjective viewpoint on a materialistic or deterministic position. It comes from the pragmatism demanded by a phenomenology unendingly and undividedly cosmic, mineral, energetic, biological, psychological, mental, cultural and social that, in all of its facets, has a significance and a function of unavoidable concreteness. When we demise one of them, we demise all of them and us all, as we are of them all.

If it is thus highly improbable that man might be a success story in the cosmic sway of evolution, it is principally because he might be too late in grasping bodily and mentally the substantial oneness of himself and the universe that contains and sustains him. He seems more alert to the moral and social evils he lavishes out than to the biophysical evils in which he burrows himself and his environment. His action on earth is more like a blind fury than anything else and he becomes ever more adroit at it. The celebration of the bicentennial should then be a beginning of "continental congruence" that on the human level includes (axiomatically) a condition of social equity.

It is not a rededication that will save this land because the premises were strangely set at the inception. For some obscure reason the interplay between the social and the natural soon got on the wrong footing and there it remained. Exploitation has been the general downgrading and one-way relation between man and nature. Exploitation of nature and man was also carried out on the man-made—the villages, the towns, the cities—exploitation until one couldn't care less about the stripped-down brutes, left as no more than depleted camping grounds for technocratic and greedy wonder boys. But people are populating those ruins, "growing" and dying in them. They are the lot who know the dark and filthy corner as the cornerstone of what is without oneself, having the within of oneself molded and warped by it.

As everything has a price, another way of saying that there are priorities, it has been quite clear now and for some time that we are incapable of pricing things. Our priorities look even more brutal than bizarre. See the five-to-one overkill capacity of the U.S. versus the U.S.S.R. (the United States is four times more peace-loving, one guesses), the one hundred million cars on the run versus dying cities and a polluted country, the glee and the glory of the Madison Avenue incantations selling alcohol, smoke, disease and irrelevance. It is not of too much avail to say many positive things have been accomplished. The wrath of social chaos is with us, both it and us contained and imprisoned in an environment that hardly ever before in the whole history of man has been more squalid; because the squalor possible in the machine age is uniquely unhuman, it is not made of worn-out objects but of obsolete things, enormous heaps of them. And the obsolete is clamoring its presence and its fraudulence. It often seems incorruptible and mortifying corruptible flesh. Crude and cruel, it makes uniquely bleak settings for sloth and dereliction.

But don't we have the splendor of surburbia? Yes, the myriads of golden cages to loneliness and quasi-biological nostalgia, the place where the cultural suicide of the wealthiest nation in history goes on. The place where repaciousness and arcadia are sold by the millions of acres. Indeed, dimness and naught are not really of the ghettos, they are of the suburbia, where the no soul, the black man clearly reads in its tenant, is.

The continent and the country need a species with a vectorial thrust. Vectoriality demands structure. Society needs co-ordinative and synthesizing efforts at the physical base of its existence that will permit its urban population to be truly urbane. Whenever such is not the case, the city becomes a Gordian knot of frustration and resentment, and its citizenry is sacrificed to chaos and physicomental exhaustion. Society needs such co-ordinative elements if it will ever be equitable with its people. Priorities are to be respected, otherwise mind and spirit are dead issues.

As the performance of architects and planners has been almost consistently irrelevant within the problem of an urbanizing civilization, I propose that a radical departure from the hopeless tangle of our urban centers seems a physical imperative, socially urgent, culturally mandatory, and historically (evolutionarily) timely.

ILLS

1. The first two hundred years have been characterized by a play of power informed by ownership and greed, not by humaneness.
2. Free enterprise has failed, socially and culturally, and has established rules of practicality at a dismally low level of realism.
3. The technological explosion has subordinated the needs of people to the tyranny of the production-consumption mystique.
4. Feasibility has all but killed desirability. Consequently, waste has become a physical and ethical dilemma.
5. Whole man has been mortified by persistently wrong priorities favoring questionable practices.
6. Expedience has characterized performance, and expediency is most of the time irrelevant for the lot of

man. With a condition of pervasive irrelevance, the social temper becomes, by necessity, fraudulent and reactionary.

7. The country has separated itself from the continent, inasmuch as it has demonstrated a cunning for the destruction of the ecological balance it lives in and by.

8. The experiment in irresponsibility that is so much part of the contemporary scene might come to a conclusion, as time for recovery is getting short, some say one generation.

## CHANGES

1. Knowledge, concrete life, is not ingrained in ownership but in use (usefulness) and the capitalistic umbrella is really that screen between the owner and reality, not owned by anyone, that has to be played down to its expediency level.

2. "Free" enterprise man has generally not the knowledge, the inclination nor the wisdom to decide how he is going to put his skills to use for his own sake and the sake of mankind. Society must help him to define its sociality together with the consciousness of the gap between the practical, with its immediate rewards and the real with its long term rewards of concreteness.

3. We cannot go on letting technology tell us what to do next. We'll have to put ends ahead of means by defining less hypocritically our aims, if we have any, and then by telling technology and science to define the means appropriate and sufficient to the task.

4. People's gullibility and attachment to things, to fragments of performance, have allowed the producer and the merchant to indulge in the irrelevant while the most down-to-earth needs go ignored (equity and congruence). That makes for a grand gross national product and a massive glut of things done because

feasible—and of things needed and not done, the doing of which is imperative.

5. The order of priorities denounces the reasons and the reality of a civilization more clearly than wealth and power. In the case of the United States, there is a clear and brutal contrast between the wealth of the nation and the pauperism of its civilization. If we want to make the individual a livelier man, we must give him (that is to say ourselves) an environment that fosters life.

6. We must come to terms with the ambiguity of the expedient. The drowning man needs a rope, not a lesson in swimming or a lecture on physical fitness or life-after-death. The rope, for the American man, is a structure that will physically afford him the urban life he seeks. It does not help to wrap this primordial need in the hypocrisy of expediency and call it social, political, economic pragmatism. Gravity thermodynamics and the ferocious demands of biology are the number one reality, the bottleneck opening on the mental kingdom. If we ignore them, we are in for obscurantism.

7. That the country be one under God might be of interest for some people. It is, though, of far more benefit to mankind if the country is one with the continent physically, biologically and mentally speaking, advancing the cause of the world at large and benefiting more from it than anything else.

8. The American experiment has had its course and its curses. It is time for adulthood where the pollution of the mind gets a good blow as much as must the pollution of the environment. Now we know we can undertake unbelievable tasks. (What good American, ten years ago, would have conceived as believable a moon shot with an eleven-second discrepancy between programming and performance—or that we

would invest three to four hundred thousand dollars per kill per person in Asia, and that in five years we would kill hundreds of thousands of "them"? And the whole in the face of widespread poverty and indigence . . . ?) It is well time we concern ourselves with tasks which might well be unbelievable because unbelievably compassionate.

## THE BIOPHYSICAL DISCIPLINE

If technological man had conscience of his dependent position in the whole of nature, he would be better equipped to do a good job for himself because in the long run, a cosmological phenomenon might put an end to the adventure of man. This phenomenon is probably in the making, and it is quite possible that man is one of the agents of this making. Disregard for nature is, in any case, the worst premise for survival, let alone development.

Whatever we do in morals, politics, philosophy, sciences, is highly irrelevant if the fundamental context of natural man is ignored. And natural man is ignored the most when nostalgia dictates. Natural man is that creature whose complexity is in constant growth (culture) and whose biological structure is an indispensable constant, morphologically quasi-stable. For such creature sociality is a second nature. He evolves within it by culture more than by biological mutation.

Natural man is a very intricate universe whose mechanisms are contained within his skin boundary, a universe in turn contained in a social-cultural and no less intricate universe, the physical and institutional body social, furthermore contained and sustained by the universe of nature. The skin of the individual defines only grossly its concreteness. He extends himself as far as his conscious and unconscious mind projects him and as far as his action reaches out in society and nature. As the individual permeates society and nature, so does society permeate the

individual and nature. The city is the instrument of this
phenomenon. Nature in turn, in its encompassing dimension, is the building material and the energetic sustenance
of both man and society. Whenever we try to cut or
separate any of those three, we kill and obliterate. That
is the equivalent of saying that if we do not come to
terms with what we are, we are not. Metaphysics cannot
shed physics and remain a constituent of the world (a
constituent of libraries, perhaps?). Equity within society
is illusory outside a congruous envelope of nature.

There is then a biophysical discipline that is imperative
for any and all organisms. At its most radical level, it is the
discipline that demands for every performance of any organism the double presence of a parameter reflecting
growing complexity and another parameter reflecting growing miniaturization. This is inescapably written in the laws
of physics, biology and sociology. The vectoriality of life
is contained in the durational flow incapsulating ever-
increasing performances (complexity) in ever-contracting
spaces (miniaturization). The absence of the miniaturizing
phase would contradict complexity, inasmuch as, in one
form or another, everything is immanently present in the
universe, but a relay taking one thousand light years'
time-space is evidently not scaled to the pace of the
thinking device that the brain is. The brain has compressed (miniaturized) the "universe" in a few pounds-
inches of space-matter-energy. Only by way of this
miraculous contraction of performances (information, communication, etc.) is the brain a concrete (willful?) process
presiding over the other miniaturized "universe" of the
body.

If the city is an organism made of all the intricate interaction of bodies physically peripatetic and demanding,
mentally diffusive and willful, then the city can only find
a reasonable chance for success within the same rules
disciplining any other living phenomena: The rule of
duration of complexification and miniaturization.

## THE PHYSICAL STRUCTURE

Those are the rules that will make concrete the advent of the truly urban society. Within this three-faceted law of duration-complexification-miniaturization is to be defined the physical structure of society. Outside of these rules are megalopoly, suburbia and segregation, identically given to entropy and naught.

As structure must precede performance, our communities, resultant of laissez-faire, are hopelessly incapable of performing their task. The absence of a functional, logistical and skeletal structure makes them futile and, at the scale they are, evil. In their flat gigantism are all the ills and devastation of an organism unfit for life. They are indeed the only flat "living" phenomenon of this earth (the vegetal is the closest approximation to "flatness" since exposure to light is its road to survival) and quite possibly of the entire universe inasmuch as two-dimensionality is essentially an abstraction of the mind. Abstractions they are, creeping everywhere in webs ever more tenuous, ever more lonely and absurd.

The physical structure for the society of man will be wrapped, by force of the concreteness of life, around vertical vectors and will form "city-miniatures" of three congruous dimensions connected to major "river cities" ribbing the continents and not suffocating them under asphalt, cement and pollution. To understand this one must see clearly the essential chain that connects matter to mind. The chain is knowledge, that imponderable but formidable stuff working by way of information (data), communication (transmission), retention (memory), manipulation (co-ordination), thinking (invention-creation) that grows out of the energy of matter by feeding on packages of energy more and more selected and concentrated (complexity and miniaturization). Again, in this chain the mineral feeds the vegetable, the vegetable feeds the animal, the animal feeds the mental and the mental will feed the social-cultural. Well, none of those could be conceivable in a diffuse, amorphous state. A contraction (miniaturization) of performance is at the outset of them all. And with them all, it moves step by step. The present step after the geological, the biological, the reflective, the mental, is the cultural-social (noosphere). For it the instrument is the congruous city, the social, miniaturized organism that, as yet, we do not have. The planner who does not grasp the inevitability of this advent is out of touch with the teaching of the geophysical and biosocial, out of touch with reality.

## THREE-DIMENSIONAL TOPOGRAPHY

As a critique by itself does not get anywhere, I must at least diagrammatically exemplify the ideas presented in the preceding. In defining a three-dimensional city, one defines a new man-made topography or landscape so co-ordinated as to contain the "inlets" and the "outlets" for the needs of the thousands of individuals composing the society. It is a plumbing system for society where physical flow and swiftness are the media in which the software of man's constitution can easily seek, find and reach those things the city promises but rarely or never delivers.

I am not advocating the miraculous, I am summarily describing the character of a complex miniaturized organism that compounds efficiency and frugality in its physical performance, freeing the mind and the soul for their tasks and flights.

It is my heterodox contention that in the priority list for the next generation is first the construction of the archetypes that after due verification will transform this continent into a congruous interworking of forces dedicated to the freeing of man's mind within a substantial and highly tempered social milieu. In this prospective, the first two hundred years were the tooling phases for such an immense undertaking, and if we do not find in this contraction-implosion the critical temperature for compassion-creation we will be swept away by the floods of population, chaos, ugliness and extravaganza, scattered in which will be, in tenuous membranes, the impotent marvels of our minds.

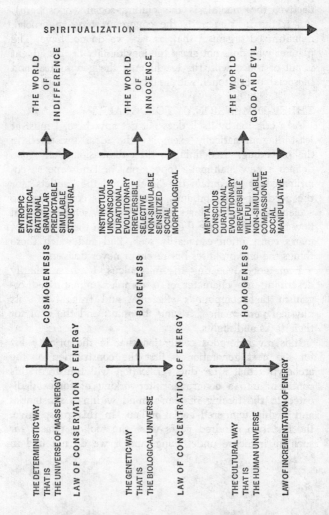

SPIRITUALIZATION ⟶

THE WORLD OF INDIFFERENCE

THE WORLD OF INNOCENCE

THE WORLD OF GOOD AND EVIL

COSMOGENESIS

ENTROPIC
STATISTICAL
RATIONAL
GRANULAR
PREDICTABLE
SIMULABLE
STRUCTURAL

BIOGENESIS

INSTINCTUAL
UNCONSCIOUS
DURATIONAL
EVOLUTIONARY
IRREVERSIBLE
SELECTIVE
NON-SIMULABLE
SENSITIZED
SOCIAL
MORPHOLOGICAL

HOMOGENESIS

MENTAL
CONSCIOUS
DURATIONAL
EVOLUTIONARY
IRREVERSIBLE
WILLFUL
NON-SIMULABLE
COMPASSIONATE
SOCIAL
MANIPULATIVE

THE DETERMINISTIC WAY
THAT IS
THE UNIVERSE OF MASS ENERGY

LAW OF CONSERVATION OF ENERGY

THE GENETIC WAY
THAT IS
THE BIOLOGICAL UNIVERSE

LAW OF CONCENTRATION OF ENERGY

THE CULTURAL WAY
THAT IS
THE HUMAN UNIVERSE

LAW OF INCREMENTATION OF ENERGY

# THE NEW ENVIRONMENT

SUMMARY

Environment is considered an element of knowledge. It is also observed that there is in man an anguish, unabatable and residual, impervious to the healing of knowledge. The agents of this residual are fate on the negative side and will on the positive.

Anguish is, nevertheless, related to information and misinformation.

There are two kinds of information: The synthetic and the environmental.

The synthetic informations, when linked one to another, tend to breed savagery in a degree related to the power they can muster and use. Misinformation breeds obscurantism. On the other hand, the environmental information becomes knowledge. That is to say, it is integrally lived, suffered. Suffered because in the end it coincides with the residual anguish. The latter is the stuff on which the truly human side of man feeds for a transfigurative act. By it structure becomes form. Such act is part of the compassion-esthetic process.

One may say that:

1. Synthetic information is, or can be, of knowledge. Environmental information is knowledge.
2. Humaneness comes from environmental information and has its resolution in the esthetogenesis of the real.
3. The aim of man is to uncover through knowledge the residual anguish and in the sufferance of it becomes a creator.

On such premises the new environment becomes a problem of "compassion-esthetics," sustained by the technological skills, ever-increasing in kind and power.

The just God of Luther is seen as instrumental to the esthetic God of Brunelleschi, the early Renaissance architect. Brunelleschi's God is a growing and ever-reaching God.

The advent of cybernation-automation, the consequent liberation of man from toil, and with it the coming of age of leisure, may see cause for:

1. The reversion of life to an electro-chemical-mechanical system fully rational but joy- and sorrow-free.
2. The advent of sloth within a humanity deprived of will and creative power.
3. A humanity fully involved in the metamorphosis of the entropic universe into a compassionate system through the estheto-genesis of things.

Among the nightmares of contemporary man, four that recur are:

1. The violence and the smothering power of the countless, whatever kind it may be.
2. The obsolescence man constructs for himself with the polished, harsh reality of science and technology.
3. The concealed or unconcealed savagery of governments and of any large power structure.
4. The loneliness gripping at the heart of every man and woman.

They are all "environmental" with a reach so great that we may see them as an unfortunate although unavoidable part of the human condition. One may wonder where remedies can be found and how applicable they may be.

## INFORMATION AND KNOWLEDGE

Because information, that is, the communication of data, seems to be at the forefront of all remedies, and because lack of information goes with ignorance, I will try to project the idea of information in relation to environment and then offer a framework that could improve things.

Is information a meaty substance or a scanty dress? To say it depends on the receptivity of the informed is a quasi-truism. But it depends ultimately on the information itself, and on its power to correlate unendingly. The validity of information is not so much measured by weight, time or space extension, but by the threads it offers for connections within the condition of man. If information offers these connections, I call it environmental information, if it is incapable of them, I call it synthetic information. The psychosomatic structure of man himself defines these two kinds of information: The synthetic or abstract, on the one hand, and the environmental or "ecological," on the other. The synthetic tends to be the monopoly of the brain and is stored in its archives, whereas the environmental acts pervasively and is experienced.

After being debugged, sterilized and catalogued, synthetic information is communicated through the many channels invented by the mind. Environmental information is impervious to such treatment because it is an evolving situation more than a packaged set of data. The channels in which this information travels are the facets of environment itself and are ever-changing and dynamic. It is received bodily as much as it is received mentally.

Synthetic information, massive and instantaneous, is a quasi-miracle. Limited only by the speed of light, it will envelop the earth, in ever-shortening strands. Visual, audible, extrasensorial communication will practically abolish time as a gap between emission and reception. But the nature of such information will remain canned, "distorted," degraded, abstract, and mostly unidirectional. Abstract informations, chained one to the other, tend to produce abstract worlds. Given the chance to operate, such worlds tend toward the non-human.

## SAVAGERY

Abstraction and savagery seem linked together. The degree of abstraction from nature in the technological world tends to carry an equivalent degree of savagery. For instance, the city slums in a technological society. This may be in part because as the machine degenerates, instead of aging, it pulls in its downfall the environment itself. Based on the above observation, it might be useful for what comes later to find the difference between the machine and the tool.

The tool ages; the machine degenerates. The tool wears out; the machine breaks down. The tool is related to physiological time. That is to say, it is connected with the aging of the toiler. The machine is not related to physiological time but to identical cycles and to the eventual exhaustion of their number. Thus, the tool is closer to the ups and downs of life and is very much an organic extension of the user. It is more versatile than the machine but of limited power. The machine is tied to a given function-performance, rigid and high-powered.

The element of power and its limitless use is another factor breeding savagery when not backed by countenance. See the brutal grip of the automobile on all facets of American life: not just a killer on the highways, but a mesmerizer of culture, environment, health, grace, balance, frugality. See the smothering of Vietnam and its people under a blanket of fire and explosives.

Abstraction, especially when coupled with power, is a two-edged sword. With one edge we cut into the mysteries of the universe; with the other we bleed our kin. The synthetic information dealing with rarefied situations and endowed with powers appropriated by technology is propitious to savagery whenever the occasion arises. The synthetic information suffers from its own abstractness and more than often traps man in the strangely chaotic world of the pseudo-orderly and pseudo-complex automata.

The environmental information is formative besides being informative. It is so because it is what is called a "total experience," spatially, sensorially and temporally. The irreplaceable nature of the environmental information, or experience, defines both the importance of the environment and the tight co-ordination of space and time within the physical structure of society. The environmental information is transmitted by and through sight, sound, smell, touch, moods, light, weather, temperature, hour, and the mechanics of its performances are bounded to ecological coherence and wealth. A chaotic, squalid ecology will convey sterile informations (not considering the reaction-informations).

A lengthy survey would show, for instance, that the physical tenuity of suburbia is, by necessity, pauperizing man, notwithstanding the most sophisticated system of synthetic information available or foreseeable. In suburbia, the environmental information is reduced to a kind which is ineffectual and monochrome.

## ANGUISH

Knowledge is assimilated information. Of the total anguish to which man is captive, knowledge can conquer all but a residual, seminal and unabatable. This is the anguish that an even "perfect" society could not dispose of. Its two opposite agents are fate and will: Fate as the

*It is in the esthetic phenomenon, the estheto-genesis of things, that process and becoming can come into fusion. This is where life must tend toward to make full use of the energetic universe without being itself distracted from the swell of evolution into a mechanico-deterministic event durationally indifferent, that is to say reversible, ethically nil.*

imposition of and from the physical world on the destiny of the individual, will as the explosive and superrational power born within the living and making it a destined entity. Confronted by the brilliant and powerful working of the mind, such residual may seem all but irrelevant. But of it and in it is the ultimate nobility of man. Its power, well known to saints and autocrats, is daily redirected or perverted to the glory of diverse flags and blood types.

Of all the traits afflicting the species, this residual anguish is the most authentic, as it is unique to man and centered in him. Not so for the rationality of the mind, as this is but a refocusing of the larger and slumbering rationality of cosmos. Sufferance and joy are the truly live sounds echoing through the indifference of an immense universe, immensely powerful, immensely old, an entropic, non-human universe.

The condition of residual anguish can be touched upon only when the synthetic information is put to work within the warmer rooms of the environmental information. Then information becomes full-fledged knowledge, that is to say an integral consciousness of the condition of man, information lived and suffered, suffered indeed, as it finally refines itself into a residual of anguish. It is at this critical point that evil is reduced to its naked condition of fate. It is at this point also where the nature of man gives up in defeat or breaks its own boundaries.

## ESTHETOGENESIS

I suggest that if man breaks his own boundaries he concentrates, so to speak, his anguish on the universal suffering of the species and transfigures this suffering through the dual process of compassion-esthetics. Compassion and esthetics are the bivalent aspects of man's humaneness and cannot stand isolated from one another. Ontologically, one can say that man's aim is to uncover the residual anguish, which is that amount of suffering unconquerable by science and rationality, and in the experience of it becomes a creator: Godlike.

The ensuing process of creation is an esthetogenesis of reality. With it the nature of cosmos is ever so slowly transfigured in the nature of man, in resonance to his compassionate pleas. In this light, compassion is the articulation of anguish and comes about through the esthetogenesis of things. By way of a gross example about the meaning of residual anguish and its articulation into compassion-esthetic, a man finds apparent fulfillment in the scientific or technical world. The fate strikes him by way of personal grief, illness, accident, coercion, or a sudden passion holds him in pain and exaltation. At the hand of fate, or at the hand of love, he finds the meter of things suddenly useless and the orderly world of technical prowess redundant and scanty in one. If the challenge of deeper things does not destroy him, he will somehow touch at the nature of residual anguish. He will, in a human dimension, become "ecologically" relevant.

Then seeded by the suffering of a living set of information, the circumstances of his grief and joy, a creative process is triggered. The personal grief-joy is universalized by an expressive act: in his behavior in the family of man, or in the same work he was previously engaged in but attended with a new reverence, or in writing, music, dance, in craft or art work. When such expression is valid, it becomes the key to the door of universality and the environment and the species are made richer by it. It is to be noted that the esthetic act is such an expression and is real only when founded on this radical condition; if not, it belongs to the pseudoreality of the extravagant. In this case, the expression ceases to be esthetic because it never was compassionate.

Tragedy deals with residual anguish and as such is eminently esthetic. The melodramatic gesture is not esthetic, because it is not concerned with it, and thus the pain it deals with can find better resolution through the rationalizing process of a coherent mind.

Residual anguish is most personal because of its universality—that is to say, it touches the individual in his most private cords while being of the nature of mankind itself. It is the sacramental core of life attending to the formation of the divine. The divine is and is apprehended through the esthetic shroud. By such mediation the numbing aches are chiseled into the joy and harmony of the man-made, a neonature carving itself into the mother, but non-human, nature. The environment is container and activator of residual anguish because such anguish is eminently ecological, rooted in the species as it is and bounded by all its physical, biological and mental strands directly to the natural condition.

To repeat again, the lived or suffered information is in its residual and unabatable character eminently ecological while being eminently vexatious, and the human ecology, our environment, is to be conceived and developed within the context of man's destiny and the suffering it implies.

The surfeit of materiality and its passive if not negative hold on man's capacity for freedom makes necessary the emphatic restating of the central importance and total meaning of this element, which I see as residual and fearsome. From a religious point of view, such element is the portraiture by man of the mystery and resilience of life. I am suggesting that it has a resolution at once universal and personal and that resolution is the esthetic act in its true and only valid sense.

Thus I have moved from information to environment or total information. I have done so in the shadow of what I call residual anguish. I then said that its only resolution is in the esthetic metamorphosis.

## PLANNING AND ENVIRONMENT

If this is so, then environmental planning is an esthetic process. The technical side is the bulky one and it carries on up to the threshold of residual anguish, not a step further. There the rationalizing ends and the esthetic process takes over in full legitimacy and uniqueness. In their historical sequence, the esthetic acts constitute the esthetogenesis that man has been evolving from the beginning of his reflective life. With the advent of automation and leisure, the esthetogenesis is central more than ever and its pace may either increase exponentially or come to a stop.

In fact, cybernetics and leisure are opening three possibilities for society:

1. A world of pure rationalism, identifying man with his own machine-inventions, with an increasng obsolescence of the flesh, and with it his throbbing, his emotions, his love-misery.

2. A world of sloth governed from outside by the same electro-chemical-mechanical mind responsible for the automated efficiency, a posthuman condition extravagantly gray and fully regressive. The difference between the two is that in the first the species is assimilated into a postbiological configuration with the disappearance of the individual within the immense and self-perpetuating body of a single and undivided neoman. In the second, the species is preserved as a shadow of itself deprived of will and steered by the omnipotent technocratic fleshless maker.

3. A world intensely creative where the thirst for harmony and the commitment to frugality would see the slow emergence of anguish and strife into grace: the esthetogenesis of the real.

It is doubtful that such worlds may coexist in the way that the most contradictory conditions in civilization now coexist. Beyond a certain level of efficiency, the rational and automated world of technology may well become an irreversible process, rigidly self-contained but universal and totally ruthless. Its law, even if just, would in all probability be unmerciful and without appeal, a bloodless but bloodthirsty God, such as the Bible often presents.

In very coarse terms, one could see justice as the God of Luther and esthetic as the God of Brunelleschi. While the God of Luther is in perpetual wake at the bedside of an ailing justice, the God of Brunelleschi is the perpetual resolution of injustice into esthetic-compassion. If justice were to prevail, to become catholic (universal), then the God of Luther would move at the service of the God of Brunelleschi. But the God of Brunelleschi could not submit to Luther's God, as the whole cannot submit to the part. I see justice as protoesthetic, or the esthetic as compassionate justice.

My conclusion is thus that the aim of man is compassionate beauty. The "engineering" of such process can reap only lifelessness unless such engineering is contained in its logistical, rational and instrumental boundaries. The discourse is trying to demonstrate that the environment fails man and civilization whenever it stagnates below the esthetic threshold, yet, to distinguish the esthetic from the whimsical and the extravagant, I repeat now that the esthetic is the last resort and the resolution in one for the pervasive and fundamental inquietude of mankind.

## PROCESS AND BECOMING

How is an environment conceived? As information can be synthetic or environmental, so can the design-planning process. The synthetic design is perfected in the office, detailed and "worked out." The environmental design is begun at the drafting table and carried on as the construction develops. In the difference between the two one may see the difference between what today is called architecture and what is called sculpture or painting or jazz. In the first, the process of coming into being is only remotely influential on the definition of the object—that is, its construction. The process is coerced by the power of the mind. In the other, the process itself introduces new elements in constant flow because the becoming of the object itself is the process.

Unless planning is considered undesirable and spontaneity is considered unbecoming, the realization of an environment must be a balanced fusion of good planning and live spontaneity.

## THE PLANNED, THE SPONTANEOUS

Good planning is a technologically informed framework in which analysis and statistic, bountiful and meaningful, are the premises or the really creative task of transfiguration. By it one moves from the granular and scattered to the synthetic (synthesis) and clustered, from the unrelated and incoherent to the interconnected and coherent—not simply in the light of rationality but in the superrational light of esthetic-compassion. In the same context, the live spontaneity has to be born from a situation of joy and sorrow, reflecting an environment of promises and coherence. As spontaneity and joy are eminently personal, they work better in the details (the home, the room, the private . . .); conversely, as planning stands on numerals and extensive data, it works better for general frameworks.

All this suggests that the new environment should be planned for its broad constituents and given to free play for the individual or private elements. For the construction of the first, the most sophisticated technological know-how and the machine would be needed; for the second, the personal involvement and the tool could have the greater voice.

The first is planned, co-ordinated cybernetically, executed technologically in its skeletal framework. But it is agreeable to handcrafting. In fact, because it is made for an infrastructure one might say that handcraft is necessary for its completion. The second is handcrafted and it grows as the life within it moves.

The first kind of environment I call arcology to emphasize the complete dependence of architecture upon ecology, but not necessarily the natural ecology. In fact, what I am suggesting is that man's presence on the earth is bound to create new ecological conditions and that the sooner we will think ecologically when planning our communities the better. The arcologies are one-structure cities defining a new landscape and a new and more direct relation between the urban and the country life.

The advantages of both are retained and the disadvantages minimized. On the urban side, abundance of facilities, cultural wealth, direct contact. On the country side, direct or quick communion with nature, the open spaces, the clean air, the isolation. The scourge of commuting, the time and energy wastes, chaos and squalor are reduced to a residual.

In practice, the opposite is happening. The structure of the city is haphazardly achieved while the individual facilities are fruits of a rigid set of economic, technical, racial, religious and status standards. The result is chaos in general and dogmatism and bigotry in particular. If one adds the incoherence of the logistical organization (communication, transportation, facilities) the picture is as gloomy or gloomier than the skies of our cities. There is no need here to demonstrate the necessity of bringing man into a far greater interplay with society than any of our cities can afford by their stifled functionality.

To conclude, we are what we make of our environment. A heartless and pauper environment does nothing more than reflect and denounce the harshness and indigent condition of our minds and souls. To change all this will require greater things than wealth and determination. It will require a definite moving away from materialism, determinism and arrogance. It will require a truly reverent attitude toward the sacramentality of all things.

*It is as if the spirit of which matter is soaked, saturated, will come to life and activate itself only when exuded out of the structure of matter itself through the formidable pressure of complexification-miniaturization.*

# TOPICS

MINIATURIZATION

In a universe ruled by the laws of mass-energy and burdened by the entropic slack, any step toward complexity, complexity now centered in the power of the mind, demands a corresponding effort toward miniaturization. In a structure where the behavior of matter would be as free from the slavery of acceleration-deceleration as light is, miniaturization would possibly be unessential and the isolation of things could be not so pervasive.

The lack of understanding, for instance, is still a deficiency ingrained in the structure of our physical body, personal and social, a lack of instantaneous co-ordination of myriads of elements constructing the forthcoming act.

Miniaturization is not an end in itself but it is the inescapable bypass toward greater complexity, that is to say, human and social fullness. Within the perspective of evolution, the most pressing task of this earth's human layer is the miniaturization of the physical container it works within. Our urban systems are proto-miniaturized organisms. They are not fit for life.

## THE MAP OF DESPAIR

Population growth and affluence have suggested to planners the layout of urban and suburban systems so extensive as to cover in time a high percentage of the usable land of the earth. This is a map of despair and reminds one of the multiplying of pathogenic cells at the expense of neighboring healthy tissues. This unbalanced growth ratio on a relatively shrinking planet will kill the biosphere of the earth and man who is part of it. Nor is the killing necessary. Even the less final step of squalor and dreariness will do mankind in.

## EQUITY AND CONGRUENCE

The well-being of man and society depends on two factors: equity and congruence. Equity is a social necessity and it has been invented by man to balance his propensity for inequity. Without equity the irrational, the illogical, the unjust (also inventions of man) would be rampant. (They are.) Congruence is proto-human, human and ultra-human. It is the necessary co-ordination of the many factors performing reality, the reality that developed from an unmanned universe into a manned universe and that might be moving toward an ultra-human reality. Without congruence the structure of things falls apart, regardless of the niceties of this or that detail. Ethics, justice, power, etc. are pre-empted propositions in the vacuum of incongruence. Congruence is ecological, that is to say, it is total or it is not. Where it is not, it does not let anything else be.

## UTOPIA

The bulk of life is negated when megalopoly and suburbia are taken as the environmental bulk.

The possible condition of equity achievable in them is not validated into the ecological condition of congruence. In the present metropolitan fabric, the absence of the implosion of miniaturization makes the social organism ill-fitted for survival, let alone for development. The environment of contemporary man is a statistical utopia taken in by the game of laissez-faire. As such it tends to make man abstract.

## THE BULB OF REALITY

The real organized itself like layers in an onion bulb. Each of these is an end in itself and a means to something of greater complexity and scope. Whatever the layer, any motion toward a new synthesis (or layer) is predicated on the backing by the preceding layer: if the vegetal layer were not there to feed it, the world of the flesh would be inconceivable. Thus the species of man is not possible without the preceding animal layer. Each new layer is contained and sustained by the preceding; it is not an accidental excrescence of it.

To sustain the next step in the development of sentient and reflective life (the noosphere of Teilhard de Chardin), man shall have to put order to his own layer; he must structuralize his environment.

The second step will be the ultra-structure he will create out of such environment and himself. To put structure in his environment he must define a neo-nature, a physico-mineral sub-layer apt, as nature is not, to render him specific and solely human services. This neo-nature, necessarily rooted into the geological and puncturing through the biological (biosphere), must be congruous with the general trend of evolution so as to be one of its makers. It must then be, by necessity, of a miniaturizing character. Abstract utopia with its map of despair is the only other alternative.

## STRUCTURE AND PERFORMANCE

The geological is massive.
The vegetative is extensive.
The reflective is intensive.
There is no performance, real performance, outside the

discipline defined by such structures. Forgetting those rules is to disassociate the world of man from the whole of things. To be so disassociated is to be discarded. That much we have learned about the vectorial sway of the world.

The double opacity (sprawl and pollution) that we, the mental, are interposing between the vegetative enveloping the geological and the source of its life, the sun, as if the extensive belonged to the intensive, is stifling the biosphere, that layer that makes the mental possible. By intruding massively into the performance of the vegetative, we are endangering the future of the species and at the same time we do not structuralize the mental through the miniaturization of neo-nature, remaining thus on the pauper side of reflection.

If we do not face those constraints, we are simply dismissing any trace of compassion toward ourselves and the blunder of our species will even go unnoticed notwithstanding its oceanic bleeding throughout its short history.

## LIFE IS IN THE THICK OF THINGS

The thick of things well expresses the centeredness of life. One of the barriers the vegetative was unable to break through has been the veneer nature of its mechanism. As light is essential to the photosynthetic process, the vegetal world has to direct its skills to those kinds of patterns that will expose the maximum skin and need the minimum volume. Even in the forest the above-ground structure is the clever dimensioning and orientation of sensitive veneers to the maximum light available. In the animal life the ratio skin to volume is reversed: minimal skin to maximum volume. The energetic process is interiorized thanks to the high concentration of energy packages (miniaturization) feeding it. The animal has in the brain its most miniaturized center of power. It is from such an ultra-packaged universe that the mind can operate and reach to the outer limits of the possible.

It is as if step by step evolution would take account of itself and make a complete synopsis (miniaturization) of its achievements in order to have at its finger tips all the available power for the next leap, demonstrating that the container of universality, or wholeness, must be the miniaturization of the best instruments available.

In the social context it is inevitable that the collective making of the species has to be constructed in a "cranial box" that is the miniaturized synthesis of the human ecology.

Compression produces reach (for instance the internal combustion engine). The utter compression of the brain (miniaturization) engenders the limitless reach of the mind. Similarly the miniaturization of the urban system will cause the explosion of its creativity.

## THE ORGANISM OF ONE THOUSAND BRAINS

The mind of the city is composed of thousands of peripatetic particles all operating from individual brains. In addition to this multiplicity of wills posturing themselves in collective veneers oriented toward the light (see the vegetal kingdom), there will be a centralized brain of non-biological character (unless technology allies itself to biology and medicine and brings the computer "science" back to the ancestral father: the organic). This brain center will *only* direct the servosystems of the city.

Then the phenomenon of the city, a congruent humanized micro-universe sustained by the neo-natural layer (the physical structure of the city), is an ultra-complex organism whose centralized brain is the instrument that works at the satisfaction of the thousands of epidermal individual minds bound together by the forces of sociality and culture.

## YESTERDAY'S CITY AND TODAY'S REALITY

The evolution of the one-layer city has been brought to an end by the rubber wheel. It all might be for the best.

Ultimate absurdity at times opens the door on greater coherence. The city of today is of the past as is the instrument that has killed it. The car will be put to pasture where it rightly belongs. The city, shown its anachronisms, will seek its congruence within the ecological system of nature. Such congruence is the implosive miniaturization of the utopia of ecumenopoly accepting the neo-natural topography that reaches up to hundreds of layers into the thick of things.

## ARCOLOGY, THE CITY IN THE IMAGE OF MAN

The ecological character of true architecture is to be affirmed if the utopia of ecumenopoly is to be stopped. The wholeness of neo-nature is dependent on the wholeness of nature. They both must move within the sphere of congruence according to the structure they belong to: extensity for nature, intensity for neo-nature.

Arcology is intensively ecological and because of its self-containment is able to be integrally accepted by the natural ecology. It is a belonging of performance, not a belonging of parasitism.

## 13 QUESTIONS ON ARCOLOGY

Arcology (architecture and ecology) is the name adopted to identify a structure which is (somehow) a three-dimensional landscape or topography. In it, not on it as it is for a "natural" landscape, are organized the private and public institutions that go into making any urban center worthy of the term.

Arcologies are architectural organisms of such character and dimensions as to be ecologically relevant.

They are that architecture which is the "ecology" of reflective life.

In the genesis of neo-matter (technology), in the face of population growth and because of the complexification inherent to life development, it has become an immediate necessity that the nodular nature of civilization, represented by the "city," moves toward the hyper-density possible by a truly three-dimensional evolution: upward for the living, downward for the automated services and production (in the seas the distinction will be less definitive).

Among the many questions on arcologies arising from the audience during seminars and lectures, the following are most often asked. My answers are scattered among the papers presented in this book. What is written here under each question as an answer is far from being comprehensive or conclusive, but I think it is valid and helpful.

1. *Are arcologies technically feasible?*

Aside from the acknowledged and demonstrated fact that we build multi-storied buildings reaching up to a hundred stories, which answer the technical question inasmuch as many of the examples given are well below that height, there is a far more important side to the question. It reads: Can we afford to squander our technological wealth for things which are technically feasible but humanly irrelevant or bad, and can we honestly shy away from those things that are humanly desirable although technically demanding? If feasibility does not travel on the momentum of desirability, it is fraudulent and we all pay a toll for it.

On both scores of feasibility and desirability, arcology stands on good grounds, to say the least (see further).

2. *Are the arcologies human?*

This question is hard to answer in a few sentences, since it implies an acknowledged common ground as to what is or is not human. In the long run, that which fosters humanness is human. That is to say, a certain character of a society that makes it successful not simply as a surviving phenomenon but as a live and compassionate one. This entails a sharp distinction between the practicality of the short perspective, which often dooms the future, and the long-term realistic response to the challenges of the present.

If, for the sake of understanding, we divide the activities of man into two kinds, the service-maintenance and the productive-leisure kind, we can say that the first group tends to be of the less desirable kind, the kind which entails toil or drudgery and unpleasantness. Any organizational and structural device which will cut into the bulk and the operational side of it, will by definition render the condition of man more human. To come down to specifics; if a city finds ways of cutting the bulk of its services, including the bureaucratic machinery governing it, to, let's say, 25 per cent of it, then this city is a better place to live in as it can deliver more with less.

An incomplete list of the services:
1. Transportation systems: hardware and people
2. Transportation distribution of energy and information
3. Delivery of water, gas, power
4. Delivery of foodstuff, mail, parcels
5. Retrieval of waste, garbage and litter
6. Retrieval-collection of storm water
7. Maintenance service (the bulkiest of them all)
8. Policing and control, law enforcement
9. Fire-prevention services

A cut to 25 per cent of the former bulk of all these would mean definitely two things:

A. Move the city from indigence to wealth.

B. Cut 75 per cent off the number of people compelled to activities of a not-so-kind nature and free them for a more promising life. The observation that people would be put out of work is untenable as it really says that we must perpetuate inefficiency, that is to say, waste, pollution, ugliness, sterility, unfitness, for the sake of keeping people busy.

Arcology, because of its fundamental premises (Questions 5 and 6), is the "kind of city" which specifically can produce this deflation of the service-administration-bu-reaucracy machinery; which brings us straight into the next question.

3. *Is arcology in the human scale?*

We are unbelievably lenient toward the conditions which trap each one of us day in and day out. We think nothing of investing about one sixth of our energies and know-how in keeping us moving (the automobile). We give endless hours of our lives to connect with other things, other places, other people. We accept frustration, curtail-ments, segregation, pollution, bankruptcy (inner cities) to the glory of the sacred cow we call affluence, and we un-consciously accept the townscape and the cityscape as of human scale. The fact that we do not usually perceive the enormous size of the environment we make comes back to us with vindictive force. We literally waste away inside gigantic pancakes of sluggishness and confusion, noise and pollution, of quite a flagrantly inhuman kind.

What I propose is the complete opposite. It is a rela-tively large, three-dimensional structure which is a fraction of the total bulk of an equivalent flat city. A phoenix, which instead of encroaching on good farm land for 200–300 square miles, stands identifiable, positive, comprehen-sible, bold and efficiently performing (Question 2) on 3–4 square miles in a sea of public grounds and parks.

The true meaning of scale is in the responsiveness of a certain instrument, structure, space to the human needs. It is not in visual familiarity, as this is indiscriminative be-cause, most of the time, it is forced upon us from child-hood, and must be considered objectively and when neces-sary modified. Familiarity, the habitual, is not necessarily the desirable, the human.

4. *Is arcology a priority or a luxury?*

If the two preceding questions were satisfactorily an-swered, the top priority of arcology should be clear. In the sense that grace is the extreme luxury of being alive to

the hilt, arcology, as anything else, better be *for* luxury.
The fine tuning into the context of things is the wealth afforded by the evolutionary process. Let us remember that
its inception was scant, dull, torpid, blind, out of the en-
nui of matter, endlessly repackaging itself in hopelessly
segregated monads. How luxuriant, in comparison, is the
bio-mental reality of the present. If by luxury we intend
the opulence in which a minority of the human family
dwells and operates, then the priority of grace becomes
indispensable. We will not solve any problems at all, be
they political, social, spiritual, economic, unless our house
is in some order and makes some sense structurally, logisti-
cally, physically, morphologically. That is to say, it must
take a coherent position within the ongoing genesis of the
real (evolution at its present existential stage).

5. *Is miniaturization equivalent to stress?*

Yes, definitely. One need only look into life and into
non-life to understand where stress is and where it is not.
What qualifies the case is the "positive" or "negative"
sense of the stresses, or better how the stresses are inter-
acted and most fundamentally what is the number of
those inner interactions at any given moment. The number of stresses within a human brain is billions of times
greater than the number of stresses in the brain of a digit
computer.

Does that leave us any choice between macro-technol-
ogy and mini-technology (microbiology)? Miniaturization
is nothing else than the spatial arrangement that consents
this inconceivable number of stresses to exist and to organize themselves in "constructive" responses. What is true at
the level of a single organism (made up of myriads of participatory units, the cells) is, to a degree, true for an "organism" made of participatory individuals. To de-stress
society is to unwind its mechanism. This can be carried
out to the lower limits of social stress and co-operation
where the only mode of exchange is money, a symbol but

only a symbol of a supposed co-operation. Miniaturization is not a process of giving up. It is an inclusive process inasmuch as it is a physical condition that keeps things and events "together" so as to make them perform and achieve.

Miniaturization is not the shrinking of a bed or a closet, nor the scaling down of a living room or terrace. It is the expulsion of those elements that go for the chastising of the urban landscape and the punishment of its dwellers, as the time and space gaps present in the challenge-response mechanism of any organism is an existential punishment imposed upon it. By expelling, for instance, the car and the paraphernalia of its demands, 50–60 per cent of the urban topography, and a better organizing (three dimensionally) of what is left, one can add to this physical reduction of the cityscape the physico-functional reduction spoken of in answer No. 2. At that point, miniaturization leaves the field of pure opportunism and becomes an ethical imperative. Miniaturization as an ethical imperative, far from being paradoxical or absurd, is quite simply the need for the conscious use of the universe of matter and energy, by the living phenomenon, in the only way that can confer to and maintain in it survival and evolutionary traits.

6. *Would people living in an arcology lose their identity?*

The reality and identity of the person is only to be found in the context of society and history. Without society man would have disappeared eons ago. Without history society would be a fossil case not unlike the ant or the scorpion. That is to say, man is essentially a co-operative animal and a cultural animal (there is not such a thing as the culture of one). In the life of the species, co-operation far outpaces, outdoes, outweighs antagonism, enmity and anarchy. It is more than virtue out of necessity. It is, fundamentally, that the whole (the family of man) is far more than the sum of its parts, and this "more" is invested into the person whose making is then not just genetic but is also cultured, civilized, social, religious, compassionate. We become more ourselves the more we become collectively relevant (not, by the way, powerful in tonnage or energy consumption). If the preceding answers hold true, then inescapably the well-conceived arcology offers, by far, the best platform for self-fulfillment.

7. *What of waste and pollution?*

If we call a unit of achievement a "quantitative" measure of performance per unit of energy "consumed," then a process is more wasteful the more energy is expended to carry it on. It is in most cases also proportionately more pollutant. Waste and pollution are therefore the negative image of frugality. The less frugal is a system, the more wasteful and the more pollutant it will be.

As for the specific problem of waste collection and disposal, once such waste has been reduced to a minimum by the power of frugality, it is quite clear that inherent to the arcological pattern is the ability common to any complex, miniaturized system to dispose of its own waste product effectively and thoroughly, in contrast to the ever-failing attempts made by the complicated, gigantic and congested urban structure of today where distribution and retrieval assume aspects of paroxysm and at times of surrealistic fantasies. If in doubt, one has only to follow, temporally and spatially, the vagaries of any of the millions of manufactured or manipulated goods we sustain ourselves with. Follow them from their origin as raw materials to their discarding as junk or litter. What a fantastic voyage and how much absurdity. It is even more distressing to follow the manipulated man in his odysseys.

8. *Political and economic aspects?*

Of all the pressures exerted upon society, the political and economic, though diverse in nature, have comparable blind drives, blind in the sense of self-contradictory. Reform to them might well have to come from even more driving forces. That is to say, not from within the political or economic body but from outside them. That is how technology is operating right now. It will be unfortunate for man if politics and economics will be technocratically redefined (Fuller?). It would be from bad to worse even if a higher degree of equity might result in the process. The reason is pretty stark: politics, economics and technological structures, from administration to production, are and must be kept where they belong, within the instrumental context. Whenever they become normative and final, they encroach on a world they cannot comprehend and thus cannot direct. Free enterprise might be a case in point. What does "free" stand for? Free from malice, from greed, from coercion, from intolerance, from paternalism, from monopolization? Addicted to them. Addicted enterprise is a truer characterization. The normative "free" is fraudulently wrapped around a court of minor and major private and corporate operations not exempt from fraud themselves. The less controllable, the more politically and "lawfully" covered they are. It might be important to observe here that authority must be "powerless" to be real. Authority has the power of conviction. Authoritarianism has the power of coercion. Authority is knowledge. Authoritarianism is arrogance-fraudulence.

Only a total subordination of the technologies of government and economics to the ethical demands of society can win for all men a better condition. This must come about regardless of the environmental context we will be in. To worry what a certain physical change might do to our ill-fated institutions is misdirecting our concern. It might well be that the major gain to be gotten from arcology, as if from a healthy mutation, is the radical reform of our economic and political structures. To prognosticate what the changes will be is to pretend a clairvoyance that we do not have. Our politicians and economists cannot tell us what next year will bring, let alone next century. Does the composer who acquires a new instrument (the arcological structure) know what his compositions are going to be?

9. *Can arcology fit within an existing city?*

Yes, inasmuch as something healthier can supplant a decaying organism. It would depend upon the relative size and power of the two systems. It would depend upon the autonomous power given to the arcology and to its ability to control its own buffer zone: the open spaces belonging to its inhabitants. It would depend on the quality and substance of its linkage to the city and the country. It would depend essentially on the inner quality of the arcology itself reflected by the liveliness of the society developing in it. One clearly positive aspect is the almost 50 per cent reduction of "dislocation" of population from the dislocation in a comparable urban renewal project. This is so because the building site for arcology is minimal, which means practically no dislocation of population in the construction phase of the arcology.

10. *What about change and expansion?*

It is definitely true that it is easier to tear down a neighborhood and put a freeway through it than to transform the skeletal sysem of an existing arcology to allow for drastic changes. What is to be understood is, however, that a neighborhood, cast among the unplanned, unresponsive, regressive, metropolitan pattern, is constantly submitted to the vagaries of the almost fatal capriciousness of the "free enterprise" dogmas and as such is by definition a non-working structure. (See Question 8.) The mortgage on the life of each city dweller defined by the mortgage-obsolescence of the environment that makes up his life is the *causa prima* and the mandatory demand for change. In human terms this kind of change is better termed as the disruption of a certain condition of poor "standard" so as to install in its place another condition which standard is intrinsically as poor but that makes for a financial dynamism, hardly percolating "down" into the condition of man. That it might be easier to undo badness than it is to undo lesser badness is quite right. Chaos is more easily "substituted" by something else. The "sin" is in the pragmatic acceptance of a disposable badness, as what makes up such badness is our own lives.

Where the real difference lies however is in the fact that a frugal system is, by definition, more easily altered, readapted, than a non-frugal one. One might rebut that. We deal not with two systems, but with a system and an a-system. The metropolitan disintegrated structure is a-systematic in the sense of being randomly, casually defined. But what goes for order in the mineral world, the atomistic-statistic order, is proto- or sub-order in the world of thought and consciousness. It is this short-changing that we perpetrate for ourselves that makes the environment of our making sub- or proto-human. It is a question of responsibility. Faceless responsibility is sub-responsibility and well fits sub-human (sub) systems.

That is how what belongs to the public, the collective patrimony, ends up to be wasteland, the parking lots of our stowed-away longing. Expansion on waste land by a socially and culturally wasted soul is hardly "growth." It is a firmer grip of sub-planning on the affairs of man. In ontological terms it is fate taking the upper hand (statistically driven) at the core of (urban) life. It is again the wisdom of nature which points the way. The fitness of any living system is stringently gauged to the size of it.

Gigantism is a threshold to annihilation, for at least one clear reason: When the environmental challenges are not responded to swiftly and coherently, the necessary interdependence of organism and environment break down. Sluggishness, dumbness, desensitization, retardation characterize bigness in nature as well as in corporate structures. The largest and most complex non-biological systems are the metropolitan centers. To suppose or think that accretion into a bigger and bigger conglomerate is to the advantage of the system is to think against our best knowledge. For any community there is a visible or invisible boundary for the optimal life of its citizenry. As it is for a person, growth is physical in the initial phase and then it becomes inner growth of a non-physical kind, so it should be for the structures that sustain our development from conception to grave. The same mechanism that perpetuates life and injects in it the element of novelty (the conception and birth of the new organism, from parents, physiologically developed) applies to the conception-birth-development and the appearance of offspring in the urban field. Both phenomena deal with the manipulation of matter and energy by a drive of a higher order, life. More than an analogy is the re-enactment of a similar upsurge of the yeast of life at a different level of intensity and consciousness and consequently, of complexity.

The city is comprehensive of the single organism. The single organism is not comprehensive but participatory of the city. The size of any "organism" might well be defined by the power of interiorization. The greater such power, the more comprehensive (larger) the organism can be.

11. *Is arcology isolated or isolating?*

To put boundaries to a phenomenon is not to isolate it. It is to be able to govern, serve, care, identify, characterize it. Isolation comes from division, sub-division, not from containment, self-containment. As we cannot define as living an organism dismembered and thrown to the four winds, we cannot count for qualitative life in an "organism" which responds to demographic pressures by splashing out further and further and which, because of the resulting imbalance, has to slash its own flesh with ever more isolating channels of "communication" and transportation.

Logistics has, as miniaturization does, and one is the implementation of the other, an ethical imperative tagged to it. The sooner we come to see it the better off we will be. A self-reliant community is an outgoing community. It has too much to give to want to seal itself off. In fact, the core result of physical containment is metaphysical radiance. By the yardstick of the mineral world, this is the radiance that is broadcast at different intensities by any living thing from as low down as the virus to as high up as man.

## 12. Why go up?

Arcology is the environmental consequence of the discovery that has found the direct relationship between the intensity of a living phenomenon, an organism, or a society of organisms and the complexity of the same. This relationship is framed, so to speak, in a physical structure which is ever more effective, the closer its dimension is to zero. The omnipresent, omniscient "point" is the seat of godliness. This is a way of saying that pure spirit has no physical dimension, or for a materialist-agnostic that spirit is not, as spirit has not physical dimensions. The closest approximation to this hypothetical pure spirit is the mind of man, whose physical dimension is man, his opus and the whole of cosmos but whose center of operation is the brain. It is a little as if the "cosmic constituency" had delegations representing it in each house of representatives we call the brain. The more distant and remote the represented, the less voting weight in the representative. There is then an implosive charge toward the center magnet we call the brain that only death or illness might diffuse. The delegates present their cases and patiently wait for responses. The delegates from the physiological individual belonging to a brain have precedence. The representative from a burned finger finds (gets) instant audience and the healing measures go immediately into effect. In converse, a star horoscope might find deaf ears (until some accident or coincidence).

Mysticisms break the rules and the boundaries of the animal recede in space and time beyond the limits of understanding. The physical characteristic of the "miracle-brain" is not smallness but miniaturization. The difference between the two is the degree of complexity.

A grain of sand is smaller than the brain, but a thousand cubic yards of sand are still and forever hopelessly simple in comparison. At the end that is why all the cubic yardage of a galaxy ill compares with a few pounds of gray matter and, by the way, that is why etherealization is the most implosive-explosive phenomenon of reality. Implosive in its process of constructing to itself the most centered-complex tools; explosive in the reach such tools are delivering to it. Well, the tool of etherealization is complex-miniaturized. That is, physically folded upon itself in the most compact, unobtrusive package.

To go up with our cities is to apply the very same technology to an analogous phenomenon. The complex-miniaturized city is the truly organic, congruous to nature, events carrying etherealization into the body social and the environment it defines for its own engrossment.

13. *What of today's cities?*

Because the cities represent a huge investment of human ingenuity and toil, and because they are the only thing we have to work with, they are indispensable for carrying on the business of life. But even for a stagnant society, cities would be in constant need of renovation and adaptation. In fact, by being so crudely conceived and so run-down, they demand far too large a share of our means and minds to just stay on the brink of collapse. We cannot afford to take care of them and at the same time we cannot afford to dispose of them. The urban crisis is here to stay for a long, long time.

For a problem of such massiveness and such future mortgaging, the least intelligent and realistic thing we can do is to do what we do: some sort of domino-theory application in reverse. If we let collapse areas and institutions which are sufficiently far apart, the corpse will retain some sort of configuration and with it a semblance of life. We will never get ahead of the game, in a game whose chips are soulful persons. The maintenance of a status quo is the most we can hope for in the existing cities, but that does not speak for any kind of acceptable future. The future belongs to bold integrals incorporating technological, logistical, funtional updatedness for which the measure of things is the meter of man, ecologically sound and spiritually alive.

As it is in the nature of evolutionary reality, those systems will survive and develop that are best suited for the challenges posed to life by the scenarios defined by the past. It is up to us to define by the means and within the rules of the physical universe those alterations in the past scenarios as to foster the developments of more human cityscapes. If those will really be so, no tears will be shed for the progressive withering away of our towns and cities. Or better, for their reach to a new sense of effectiveness there will be rejoicing not sadness or resentment. The transformism of the whole of reality is the most tangible of all intangibles. A cinematic time-compression of the development of any urban structure shows this clearly. Stone, brick, wood, asphalt, concrete become as ubiquitous as water. In and out they come and go defining and redefining the landscape of social and cultural man. Their time schedule is the life span of civilizations fitting with those within the larger time beat of a slowly, ever so slowly, aging earth and solar system. We are not the innocent savages of eons past. We are the sophisticated barbarians of the present. The nature we give to ourselves is the nature of urban man. We are born genetically "innocent" but culturally loaded.

# FUNCTION FOLLOWS FORM
## (Structure Before Performance)

The way biological life develops into new forms and consciousness seems to confirm that the instrument has a chronological precedence over the performance. An organism does not willfully construct for himself a new organ so as to attain a certain goal, but stumbles by mutant chance onto a certain characterization given to it fractionally and in infinitesimal doses. It is the fixation of such mutant novelty—the new instrument—that makes the organism able to perform a certain act which could not have been performed before, no matter how great its usefulness or how intense the desire had been for it (see the urban parallel). As such changes happen to increase his chances for survival, they increase also the number of offspring carrying the mutant alteration. The neck of the giraffe does not grow out of the will of the animal, but out of a sequence of genetic variations accidentally useful for his well-being. The function does not originate the form. It maintains it. The long neck of the giraffe is incorporated into the species in as much as it has found a function useful for the animal. At the same time, the chain of offspring of the tennis player will not show any disproportion between right and left arm though he himself might exhibit a right arm more muscular and heavy than the left, (acquired specialization in a "fringe" function, not genetic alteration working at the core of survival). If a tyrant dynasty was to demand superchampions from a restricted caste, then the genetic machine would start working (as in the case of selected cattle breeds), or else the genealogical trees of many tennis players' families would be truncated.

There is an element of pure novelty in the progression of links where the new, if accidental, instrument (mutant character) almost forces upon the organism a new kind of relationship with the environment (and with himself in the case of consciousness-reflection). It is the reversal of the abuse "form follows function" formula. It is instead "function follows form," or one can say, "structure precedes performance." The form is there in the genetic emergent mutation, a structure that appears and becomes filled with events. The earth itself is the most comprehensive case in point. It is hard to believe (unacceptable) that its "function" was the generation and sustenance of life.

## THE ESTHETIC AND THE EXTRAVAGANT

Can what is done haphazardly in the genetic world be done consciously and willfully in the mental universe? The esthetic "process" does this as it is that kind of event which justifies itself by its own advent, and its usefulness is not to be found in an a priori functional demand. And as it is for the mutant gene, it is more than often, preponderantly, a regressive mutant, the "extravagant." But now and then the extravagant is pushed aside and creation comes to be and with it the emergence within the species of a new consciousness, a new fragment of etherealization. Thus, in a way in the human world, the mutant

*Our wealth goes and is in steel and ball bearings, in alcohol and model homes, in asphalt and advertisements, in burnt oil and gross national pollution. What will be of our children? Will they be steel and ball bearings?*

accident is substituted by the esthetic event moving the evolutionary thrust from the genetic-biological to the cultural-personal. Of all other activities of man, none seem to be so clearly connecting the past to the future without passing through the purgatory of instrumentalization.

And as it happens in the biological world, often such instrumentalization gives results that are the equivalent of a (non-accidental) bad mutation making the organism less well equipped for survival. A classic example is the automobile. The survival of the race is jeopardized by the mutant incorporating the car into the structure of society. Nor is the analogy too farfetched if one considers (1) the species is in many ways an organism composed not of cells but of persons; and that (2) this organism has transferred most of its evolutionary thrust from biogenetic devices to technological tools. What remains to be seen is if the will or the discriminative power belonging to the single components—the person—has in itself retained or incorporated the ability to distinguish the good from the bad tool (mutant) which is, in human terms, the choice of life or death for the species. Only "intelligent" decisions can disengage the species from the pressure and the fatality of "natural" selection.

In the formula "form follows function" is buried the frightful fact that a high percentage of the functions are the equivalent of behavior originating from bad genetic mutations, those for instance of the "can do, thus must do" ethic (see the automobile). When the feasible becomes the desirable in as much as it swells the gross national or personal product, the mutation it stands for is not a logical or constructive mutation. Chances are that it is one of those fatally bad mutations crowded with dark forebodings.

## FUNCTIONAL COHERENCE

What is then the difference between the invention of the

*The existence of God is hypothetical if not impossible because of the diffusion operative in the universe.*
*If the implosion of the universe is "orderly," willfully evolved, there is where God may come to be (esthetogenesis).*

car and the invention of the spoon or of the arcology? To
find it one must carry the conditions they advocate to their
ultimate consequences. What appears in the automobile
context is that those consequences are the negation of the
premises on which the invention (mutation) was incorporated into the body-social. The communication-informa-
tion aim, original to the invention of the automobile, is
stunted and finally disappearing as the automobile takes
over and paralyzes society. (If the giraffe's neck doesn't
stop growing, it will make the animal unfit.) The mystique
which is at the driver's seat of this paradox can hardly be
found in the spoon, which will remain more or less always
a humble device for feeding ourselves.

The arcology? In its most naked purpose arcology is an
attempt as much as and far more than the automobile at
giving the person the swiftest way to communication, information and action. It wants to enlarge the personal universe of each individual by centering him in the thick of
things. At its most "absurd" limit, the arcology becomes
punctiform; that is to say, it contains in "no space" the
whole of itself and the organisms it is meant to serve. It
resolves itself and its own content into pure spirit. This
transformation, as paradoxical as it might appear, is none
but the dreamed omnipotence and omnipresence of God.
Civitate Dei becoming Godlike . . . God himself. The infinite complexity of a being utterly centered upon itself
infinitely powerful and infinitely wise (by definition as it
is spirit); a Point whose next metamorphosis could be the
advent of the explosion known as the "big bang," initiating
a new cosmos, the spiritual universe. A universe, liberated
from the "slavery" of mass-energy-speed, can perform
explosively instead of necessitating the implosive performance (the necessary liberating form).

So what we see on one side is the car, scattering ever-
more, to a uniform dullness and dumbness, the species of
man into isolated, segregated, electronically plugged-in

cells; and on the other, the arcology that puts each city dweller at the "center" of the city, the ideal position for a person to be conscious and to be part of the information-communication-action-participation world, to which he belongs as a social-cultural individual.

It is to be pointed out that at the service level, smallness, co-ordination and efficiency induce self-effacement. If a Cleveland needs a police force of four to five thousand, an arcological Cleveland can do with 20 per cent of that number. So it is for the other servo-systems keeping the city in shape: delivery and retrieval of goods and wastes, delivery and performance of utilities and services—whether manual, mechanical or both. To seek the opposite, with the not so original contention that if the police can become so efficient the city will become a police city, is that amount of saying that it is better to make everyone into a policeman, a garbage collector, a postal employee, a truck driver, a telephone maintenance man, a doctor, a nurse, a sewer supervisor, a bus driver (a car driver?) etc. That is to say, loose man in the maze of the amorphous where life becomes random and, lastly, God's litter. Delegation of responsibilities effectively controlled by the community is the goal and the smaller the supervised body and the machinery it uses, the better off the community. This points at more than physical miniaturization. It states also that for the "same" aims, a lesser number of service men are needed. The percentage of service and maintenance people is cut to a fraction of its former number, the bureaucratic machinery shrivels to a shadow of its former self and its inertia all but disappears. Then society ripens the fruits of swiftness, response, sensitization. It becomes dynamic, without necessarily becoming mobile. (I say this here because of the mistaken identification of mobility with dynamism.) It becomes dynamic essentially because toil, drudgery and senselessness are drastically cut to size. At this point miniaturization leaves opportunism to become an imperative—the ethical imperative that demands the conscious and willful use of the universe of matter and energy in the only way that can sustain the survival and evolution of life.

The other difference between the car, the spoon and the arcology is in the possible presence or not of the esthetic in the car, the spoon and the arcology. The automobile or the spoon are or were given a very limited slot into reality; their main purpose is to serve well, to "perform honestly." To such a category belongs a "beauty" of directness and readability, a proto-esthetic firmness, untroubled, correct, rational, logical, clinical (all present in the best of our tools and equipment). For the arcology, whose scope is almost inseparable from the context of life itself if it is true that the environment is meshed in with life, the esthetic potential is boundless; that is to say, in one and the same more promising and more dangerous. The correct, the rational, the logical, the clinical, ought to give way to the corresponding transcendental twins—the "more than" (more than rational, more than logical, more than clinical), even at the risk of collapsing into the "less than." In the most pragmatic light, the worth of man is indissolubly bound to the esthetogenetic process as it is only by it (for it) that man will find himself to be the witness of a compassionate environment, worthy of reverence—an environment made of things, of live things and of persons.

One can carry on the parallel, in a garbled fashion undoubtedly, mindful that man evolves on the three fronts of genetics, technology, and creation, with the genetic statistically adopting the formula "function follows form"; and the creative working out consciously, that is, non-statistically, "forms" which define their own function. One then sees the man-giraffe whose neck is stretching (is it?); the man-technologist whose instruments—automobiles, typewriters—accumulate his power for trans-form-ism; and the man-creator on the shoulders of the two preceding, reaching up to the branches of the tree of creation whose leaves will possibly, if not improbably, bud and grow at the radiance of the three-headed creature.

In a fully responsive arcology, all three of them must be present and working. The portent is to make the whole animal (the city), with its physiological and technological instruments and with its leaves growing amply up there, into a pandemonium, a quivering, of grace, serenity, fire, joy, reverence, excitation, consciousness, expectation. To make this possible for man it is not sufficient to shelter him from pain and punishment with the help of behavioral conditioning. On the left of zero the most we can hope for is the smallest of the negative numbers: $-\frac{1}{\infty}$ as the world of the positive numbers is blocked off by zero, itself, the edge of the two watersheds of adaptations and creation. As adaptative animals, we are purely the creatures of our environment. As creators of the real world we are the agent of a trust that cannot be completely accounted for by the pristine nature of the planet supporting us.

The question arises: Is this the right time for launching into chancy endeavors in the hope that, among the many, one might turn out to be fruitful? If the attempt were a purely blind date with the future, the answer should be no, as the suffering and the deprivations are global and intense, and the stakes are frightfully central to the hypothesis of man as an animal with a future. But if (1) this last is the situation, and (2) the date is not a blind one but indeed is radically joined to the dynamics of evolution, then the unpredictability itself of the resulting "formula" might contain the best ferments for the germination of a novel reality. It might well be the best if not the only hopeful fissure that the cleavage of our problem might have to pray in, for the invention of a more human future.

We in part shape answers by better shaping instruments of which we have experience (adaptation, improvement), but at the same time we must risk a "longer neck" even if the leaves that such neck will afford were not much more than ontologically probably and auspicable. It is then not a pure case of structure before performance— "form before function"—of the genetic world, but a well-rooted start on a background of past experiences and errors, in a journey which chartering in detail would not only be nearsighted but plainly incoherent as the land to be sought is not there to be discovered but has to be invented and created along the way. Therefore, the journey is not into things existing but toward the future of which we are, ourselves, the makers, inventors, and creators. At stake is a more intense physico-spiritual becoming and stronger fulfillments for both the person and the species. And by the way, if this is not clear, the person is also, if not more so, the ghetto-bound and the hunger-stricken, for whom immediate rescue—philanthropic piety—is often less than compassionate and too often mystifying. "We" must "immediately" feed the hungry. Upon each of us is the weight of our personal hypocritical forgetfulness and the direct responsibility for the sufferance and dehumanization of the ill fed. Beyond that, our practical solutions are sugar-coated fraudulence as they only transfer within society the same "original sins" without trying to expel them from the context of human life.

# THE CRAFTSMAN AND OBSOLESCENCE

Science may rationalize the man of flesh and bone into obsolescence. Then the just, the structural, and the rational will be undisputed masters of a species freed from sorrow and deprived of joy. If so, all that goes with contemporary man is of very circumscribed meaning—a meaning simply instrumental to this historical moment in the evolutionary process.

If this is the case, the arts and crafts are among the least effective tools of such evolution, so much so as to become ontologically meaningless. To drag them along toward the future would be less than realistic.

My contention is . . .

1. That the rational world, the world of structure and justice, is a pedestal, so to speak, to life and not life itself.

2. That on such a pedestal man, the compassionate stuff of the universe, is creating, forming, a post-rational world, a world of non-obsolescent character.

3. That such world will demand a rededication of man's best effort toward a non-expedient environment.

4. That such environment will be ecologically relevant, technologically structured, esthetically formed and that the crafts and arts will be integral parts of its infrastructural modes.

5. That the freedom afforded by leisure-automation and a newly cultivated sensitivity of the individual will open ever larger slots of time and perception for him to seek valid self-expressions: not within the scanty frame of the extravagant but in the context of humaneness.

6. That the total and converging power of the species will ultimately reveal itself as an esthetogenesis of nature, transfiguring the natural into the human in human ecologies of unforeseeable power.

7. That that which distinguishes the extravagant, regressive and squalid from the esthetic, essential and lively is the fundamentally human, existential element of anguish, ignored by the extravagant, transfigured by the esthetic.

8. That the pursuit of happiness will forever fail to abate such anguish in its residual measure and that it is indeed in the metamorphosis of such anguish into esthetocompassion where man finds life worth living and, by it, the joy to be.

The following is not the orderly exposition of a thesis. It is a group of ideas hinged together. A better organization may greatly reduce the paradoxical appearance of many of them.

The seriousness of man's condition demands from each of us an earnest effort to find substance to one's action. The craftsman cannot presume a preferential treatment. If it ever happens to be that his participation in the evolution of the species is ephemeral, he had better find for himself worthier endeavors.

## OBSOLESCENCE

Obsolescence is a worrisome phenomenon for con-

*The "pool" of the possible is as rich as the logistics allow it to be. The desirable finds its way into reality if it is "desired" enough. The feasible cannot make itself desirable if it has it not within itself to be so, not even indeed the least so, when it is actualized (not real-ized).*

temporary man. The accelerating tempo in the happening of things works as a grinder, and debris of all sorts, things, concepts and conviction litter our inner and outer landscapes.

Science, on its part and in all honesty, is looking into the possibility of a future without flesh, without pain and without joy. If this is the reality of the future, it is quite evident that the days of the craftsman are numbered. But then so are the days of man as we figure him to be.

To go with the subject in a broad perspective, one may say then that the possible obsolescence of craft as objects and as "profession" is overcast by the obsolescence of man himself.

To find the validity of crafts, one may thus have to:
1. See if the scientific dream for a fleshless species is valid or not.
2. If valid, find one's peace of mind in the present, as it comes, unquestioningly (stoicism) or passively (cynicism).
3. If invalid, try to find out if for a man with a future there is any need for the enchantments of crafts.
4. If such need is found, establish the indispensability of crafts on appropriate basis.

Taking the points one at a time . . .

Point one reads: *See if the scientific dream for a fleshless species is valid or not.*

If human life fits or wishes to fit the boundaries of the rational, it would seem that once the complexities of the mind and the miracles of the body are disentangled and displayed by science and logic, a sophisticated technology will devise less wasteful containers than the expedient flesh. But are rationality and justice, once achieved, the aims of life? Could it be that justice and rationality together form the pedestal for life? That is to say, would not a just and rational world be simply a proto-humane platform for the *unfolding* of liveliness? If this were the case,

*Compassion without congruence is pure conjec-
ture because the "cardinal" (hinge) truth is
that we are faced by an impassionate universe
and we will succeed only if we work congruently with and within it.*

what could characterize liveliness? The highest characterization of humaneness in its existential condition is compassion. Compassion is not a lacrimal effusion. It is the gift to justice of insight, the gift to structure of form, the gift of intensity to the rational, and it is the personalization of the three of them with the rewards of joy and at the price of blood and tears.

On the structural frame of justice and rationality, the compassionate constructs the living fiber of humaneness.

Here there is a moving from structure, a skeleton, to a superstructure, a form. This form is the esthetic. The esthetic in this context is an infinitely deeper and more complex element than the embellishment of a functional frame. In its compassionate self, it is itself the expression of the living. It is as if the opaque uneasiness of a universe, deprived of sensitivity, was transferred to man in the form of a residual and unabatable anguish, that amount unconquerable by rationality and justice. Man would then individualize it in personal sorrows and, in a balanced mixture of universality and subjectivity, he would take hold of matter and transfigure it—moving it from the level of justice and rationality into the compassionate world of form-esthetic.

In this sense, compassion is existential justice: the just sensitized by the condition of man, an individual. I would add that the esthetic is essentialization of compassion. Thus: existential justice is essentialized in the esthetic phenomenon, or the esthetic is the essentialization of existential justice. One could thus say that the esthetogenesis of the universe is the metamorphosis to which the universe is submitted by that organ, man, the universe itself has harbored to find a resolution to his rational, just, but non-compassionate condition.

In this manner, gross and rarefied in one, I contend that man is fundamentally not rational nor just but super-rational and compassionate—esthetic. For a world constructing itself in such terms, the second point is rejected: man cannot accept a passive role in the avalanche of physical efficiency that the technocrat promises to himself and others.

Point three reads: *If the scientific dream of a fleshless species is invalid, try to find out if for a man with a future there is any need for crafts.*

As the energies of man would then be directed toward the esthetic, it follows that the crafts would be in an eminent position in the structure of society. It may be helpful to consider here the theoretical boundaries of standard production, craft work and artistic creation. As standard will soon be synonymous with computed, one could say:

1. The computed is a practical-abstract process dealing with heterogeneous materials to fulfill a practical function.

   Craft is a well-balanced and subtly arranged material underlined by function-ideas.

   Art is an expression of feeling-ideas by what might be called a sublimated material giving form to a new entity.

2. The computed is amorphous, ordered matter.

   Craft is a harmonious organizing of matter.

   Art is a transfiguration of matter.

3. The computed is true to robot (automation).

   Craft is true to feeling-materials plus intelligence-tools.

   Art is true to the urging of the spirit.

4. The computed expresses quantity and functions.

   Craft expresses quality-material and functions.

   Art expresses intangible emotion-ideas.

5. The computed is immediate economy.

   Craft is economy by harmonic action.

   Art is ultimate economy through ultimate synthesis.

6. The computed is a time-indifferent process (low-gear, high-gear).

Craft is a duration process.

Art is capable of moving out of time.

7. The computed is that which is because it functions efficiently.

Craft is that which is because it functions harmoniously.

Art is that which functions because it is.

8. The computed has no birthplace.

Craft needs a birthplace.

Art creates her own birthplace.

For an even partial validity of such distinction, it would seem that craft is somehow occupying that band of action where man has just chosen to abandon physiological evolution in favor of one that may be called extra-biological. Among the least obsolescent objects man has ever conceived are those that are somehow the direct extension of our physiological system. For instance, clothing as a second skin or as a regained fur; footwear as thickening of the foot skin; food utensils as direct extension of hand, fingers, teeth; hunting and defense tools as extensions of fists, legs . . .

The quasi-biological utensils are still here with us but they are very much the concern of standard, and soon computed, production. The man-made object has to count more and more on non-functional characters, less and less on efficiency. The reason is in the harsh truth that the machine outdoes man 100 to 1 whenever the problem is a purely logical-technical-functional one.

The battle for domain of the rational aspect of the physical world is, for the craftsman, a lost battle. Thus, the more dominating is the need of efficiency, the less is the craftsman on the side of reason. The efficiency of the machine is making the functional craftsman obsolete.

What makes the craftsman necessary to society is a particularly qualitative element to be found in the esthetic world, not in the field of the functional. Such element is very rare because, as tentatively shown, it is very demanding. Hence, the scarcity of true craftsman.

In very general terms, I would venture to say that the
most promising field for a craft is not in the instrumenta-
tion of those activities that are at the micro-end of the
physical scale, as it cannot be at the macro-end of it
either. That is to say, not the spoon or the shoe, not the
plate or the pot, the table or the chair, nor certainly the
mega-structure defining the environmental, neo-nature of
man. I would find the most rewarding action of the crafts
in the "in-between" of the two; the homemaking, the land-
scaping, the special characterization in some public facilities, schools, restaurants, shops, temples . . .

In such a frame our environment would be defined and
executed at the macro- and micro-end by the proficiency
of technology, in the in-between scale by the temperance
and sensitivity of the crafted.

Point four reads: *If the need for crafts is found, establish
                     the indispensability on appropriate basis.*

The scheme developed in the preceding would put a
greater burden on the craftsman, the direct responsibility
of defining (in part at least) the infra-structure of the
human environment. It is there where man, as a fully participating individual, can and must pursue the most precious and delicate condition of creative freedom, a condition that far outreaches rationality, logic and justice by
comprehending and going beyond them on the strength of
such comprehension.

The ever-increasing pool of leisure-energy would offer to
the craftsman-environmentalist abundant and co-operative
working forces. Then the man-made environment would
become an integrated combination of fine technological
skill carrying on, after the conceptual phase in which the
esthetic better be forcefully present, the definition of the
macro-elements: the ecological planning, public architecture, utilities, facilities; the same skill carrying on also
the production of the bulk of the micro-elements: utensils,
wearing, applicances; and the craftsman-artisan-environ-

mentalist working at homemaking and the detailed organizing of the public life.

On the strength of all this, crafts would, with art, avoid death by obsolescence. It would not be chained to needs that are today and are not tomorrow, as this applies generally to the tooling of society (car, washing machine, typewriter). Nor would it toil particularly on the repetitive making of those efficient utensils that are extensions of our biological endowments (spoon, shoe . . .). The craftsman would be the balancing element where the technical and the esthetic would meet and produce an environment in harmony with man.

We may be possibly seeking an environment of finite human characteristics to be mastered by a progressive processing of nature, as a mineral is mined and processed to "achieve" a metal condition. The wisdom of such seeking has to be proven by what humanity will make of itself.

We are moving from the "in nature of materials" to the "in nature of man." The organic movement, born as an organic reaction to the ever-greater separation of expression from the artisan skill closely interacting with materials, has had the merit of reinstating the fundamental importance of keeping man anchored to nature. This is very basic in times when nothing gives, as yet, assurance that technology is here to stay as an ecological and cosmic phenomenon. A phenomenon postulating for man a "metaphysical" condition of harmony. Yet this must be a balancing of the intellectual dogma. From dogma to bigotry the step is brief and it takes only followers to make it unavoidable.

## MATTER AND MATERIALISM

We are headed for an existence wherein materiality, short of being esthetically transfigured, will physically add to such a burden of false needs and waste as to cause pernicious anemia on the spiritual body, a progressive atrophy of its sensitivity, a pervasive dulling of its life. All this possibly within a polished and opulent civilization.

Nature, divinity and conscience, our fathers, have told us that we live poorly and that effect and cause in one, our environment, is chaotic or downright squalid. Now technology, our *enfant terrible,* is sarcastically watching the destruction of whatever little we had of order and coherence by the frantic use we make of her expensive prodigality. If all we can do is to transform materiality into materialism, the long-sought blessing of quasi-total leisure may well be a sharp turn for the worse in the history of man.

Environment speaks to us through our senses, but if it addresses its voice only to them, the buffered noises reaching our spirits will not be sufficient to sustain our efforts for betterment. A regressive humanity is a very real possibility and no gods would be too much bothered by it. The only divinity we can and must trust is the one we may be able to construct within ourselves, and this is not possible within a squalid environment.

Whether we organically set ourselves and our cities or villages within nature, or whether we conceive a man-made second nature, boldly confronting nature itself with a perhaps too premature wish of a humanized universe, we must do so as metaphysical beings and not as cunning humans divided between the pursuit of comfort and the smugness of the "foolproof." We must exist and grow as finalities, not as instruments. Not even as the instruments of highly improbable gods.

As the reticulum of roadways and fields extends to the horizon counterpointed by settlements and villages, it comes clear how at specific points the nodule of the living phenomenon will surge, rise and quiver into the expectation of the transhuman.

The skin of the earth is coalescing in a continuum of life tenuously unified by the photosynthetic process. Roaming on and in it are the intensified quanta of the animal world, here and there herded together in social phalansteries.

Then there are the human settlements made of stone and soul, one bound to the geology of the earth, the other suspensefully and fearfully leaving its moorings in short, eventful/uneventful flights. The moorings are in a constant state of metamorphosis, and aggregation is slowly supplanted by organization.

The arcology, tightly knitted after the dissolvence of the post-technological disintegration, will reverse slightly at the center to accept environments, as a premonition of a future leaving of the anchorages into the transplanetary journey after the necessary bio-technical inventions will have made man, gravity and atmosphere unbound.

While the metamorphosizing of the human settlement proceeds, the "breathing," this release at the center to form inner landscapes, goes on as the locks of the one-way evolutionary path snap behind each threshold. There is thus an alternating of contraction and release as partial events in the intensifying suction by the magnets of life into the building blocks of his ascent into spirit.

Transarcology is a mindful "organism" bound to earth for the earth's final soundings at the dawn of the esthetogenetic release.

# TRANSARCOLOGY (In Flight Above Central Europe)

These were notes occasioned by the visit to Hungary—a statement of faith, not a statement about contextual findings, as it is well imaginable; a faith which comes naturally when one is surveying on a continental scale the magnificent work of man, the agricultural wizard. There, under one's own eyes, is the man-made ecology stretching uninterrupted and cosmic in extension: a thing that in its poignancy is not only a reality sustaining man, but it is also a premonition of a transhuman future.

On the contrary, the down-to-earth Hungarian experience, superficial by circumstances, was split. On the one hand, the spirited drive of the people, and on the other, the quasi-obsessive dulling, demanded and carried on by homo economicus. Homo economicus is quite incontestably a structural part of Homo sapiens; that part which assumes the responsibility for the logistics of supply and of production-consumption-distribution. But he is an alter ego at the service of his master or he is an improbable guru for the idolatry of greed.

It is not too strange thus that the sought-after standard of living, so often and in the most disparate countries becomes the standard of not dying or dying spiritually.

The tragedy is possibly most acute for those people that find themselves operating the mechanisms of economic and social power, as it is for them that the dilemma of physical-economic improvement versus civilization results so often in environmental, social and cultural naught.

One is compelled to ask why it is that a war with an outer enemy can tap the most formidable resources and bring in results, and a war with the enemy within, mediocrism, materialism, transforms the battleground into an economic rage?

## EMERGENCY AND EMERGENCE

Because for one thing, the aims are not as clear-cut, thus the aims are not understood. Because the aims, once understood, would frighten the timid and the faint of heart. Because the quivering of emergence cannot take hold unless emergency, the critical temperature by which emergence comes into being to vivify history, is clearly declared and the consequence pursued willfully.

Emergency is a condition sine qua non for emergence. Naturally, it does not follow that the response to emergency will make a society puncture the present and launch the best of itself out into the improbable but indispensable reality of the spirit.

The emergency of survival (nation, society) is only a proto-cultural-proto-civic emergency. It is at the end and notwithstanding the horrors and heartbreaks, only an emergency of "maintenance": To maintain, for instance, the dignity and respect of a people. The wretchedness of a post-war condition tells clearly of the low rung from which one has to begin once more for the emergence. And there at the critical moment we default. Emergence soon becomes mainly an economic matter, as if the dead, the maimed, could be atoned for by the affluence of the living.

Such a bargain is crude. The price to be paid runs as brackish water in every crack and cranny of the social and environmental structure. Civilization lingers on past fullness. The joy of life, the lust of life looses itself in the obesity of the mind.

My very general and possibly unjust criticism of today's planning is that we are shortchanging ourselves once more by setting our aims far below the longings of the species.

If this is so, we stand accused of treason by default, the crime being the most general and crucial of all: the miscarriage of life in one of the cul-de-sacs history is burdened with.

By setting rings of "housing" around the city core, and by making those places economically more desirable, we set the spiral of affluence in motion. We pre-empt the heart of the city which, though incapable of competing in services (physical) and "commodities" with the new housing has or had a powerfully cultured charge. The pre-empting is in favor of a "better way of living," which is spiritually and culturally insolvent and which will be rapidly moving by reason of exponential decay (confusion, traffic, congestion, disruption, isolation) into physical bankruptcy.

We thus de-etherealize the core while "materializing" the periphery, a process which is, ontologically speaking, the exact opposite of life's struggle toward etherealization.

## DEATH BY AFFLUENCE

If we cannot reverse the process, we will engulf the society we try hard to help, into not metaphorical rings of increasing materialism, further and further away from those painfully built magnets one can still find in the

*How many of us make what we wear, what we put in our houses, what we eat, what we watch, what we listen to . . . what we think?? For most of us, and for most of our "doing," it is the access to options and manipulation that counts, not the access to production or creation. No amount of envy, wishfulness, hypocrisy, can change that.*

better-kept cities. It would seem imperative that where the institutions of civility and culture are, there should be developed adequate housing so as to intensify the urban milieu and its cultural fruits, instead of killing it by a washout. Physical desirability must be made to coincide with social and cultural desirability because that is the only way we can have a future for our communities.

In fact, economic desirability comes as a distant third, as it can be only an instrument for the evolving of the other two. Nor can we delude ourselves into being able to multiply by "reproduction" the most difficult of all contexts: the urban environment.

This can happen only slowly and be of the times only within an arcological structure where the complete integration and integrity of the community is sustained by a no less integrated and integral context. Nor can any degree of electronic sophistication by itself be a substitute for an intensely alive urban core. There is a difference of nature between the two and in a confrontation (sterile and unnecessary) the electronic city comes far, far behind as a pale and brittle second best.

The double problem of materialization of the human environment and the limitation to a precious few centers of fully vibrant cityscapes that one can optimistically anticipate is a dark and foreboding vision of things to come. It somehow sets the most degrading of the American "miracle," the goal and the state of opulence as the mirage and driving force for the less wealthy or "developed" countries. I, for one, wish those countries better luck and loftier goals for the sake of all mankind.

*We have made the barbarous mistake of identifying process with becoming. The confusion is killing us and civilization. The production-consumption carnival has put process on the altar. Process, not becoming, is the business of business and the business of ecological debacle. Becoming, on the other hand, is incapable of destruction, inasmuch as becoming is the antithesis of un-becoming. The opulent society is un-becoming.*

This short paper does not contain even the beginning of an answer, but it suggests a direction. It is the direction of implosion as against the direction of explosion.

The choices are really two:

1. The Frugal: The instrumentality for the services of society are imploded and consequently the mental and spiritual options "explode" and man steps up one more flight toward the spirit.
2. The Opulent: The instrumentality for the services of society explode (United States) and consequently the mental and spiritual options wither and man steps down toward matter (materialism).

## THE SEED

*The vegetal, the animal, the human and the social seed originate a cycle of gathering and organizing matter in a progressively complex and responsive organism.*

## THE LIVING

*The living is then a co-operative process not a disintegrative one (death). It is an implosive process, not an explosive one. It is a miniaturization process favoring the ever more complex interactions making the becoming.*

## THEREFORE

1. *In any given system, the liveliest quantum is also the most complex.*
2. *In any given system, the most complex quantum is also the most miniaturized.*

# A CANADIAN ALTERNATIVE?

Let us consider two aspects of the Canadian context:
1. The agricultural productivity and the farmers' isolation.
2. The urban structure with the urbanized society that lives in it.

Let us view them in a light which is not common, but which I find more than just plausible and in fact revealing.

1. *Agriculture*

Canada is one of the most massive assembly-line producers of cereal (wheat). A peculiar kind of assembly line, indeed, but indisputably one.

The selected seeds (assembly-line produced) are sowed in strictly controlled ways and patterned at the beginning of a production cycle, well structured and scheduled.

In agriculture, the assembly-line attendant is not the farmer. The farmer is the supervisor. The attendants are the genetic codes of the plants cultivated and the climate, having as workbench the soil, and for materials, the minerals, solar energy and water. The inner trust of the seed is the force that reaches out and captures them,

organizing (imploding) the captives according to the
genetic pattern hidden within.

One sees a peculiar thing in this kind of assembly line:
the product is a more etherealized stuff than the attendant
climate and the materials going into its production. The
biological is formed out of the mineral world and physical
energy: from matter to life. This is at least partially the
inverse of the technological assembly line where human
"stuff," the attendants, are "consuming" themselves in the
production of a hardware; that is to say, from etherealization to materialization. The following diagram shows the
parallel:

|  | Farming Assembly Line | Industrial Assembly Line |
|---|---|---|
| Ends | FOODSTUFF | HARDWARE |
| Media | SOIL, ENERGY | RAW MATERIALS, ENERGY |
| Attendant | SEED'S CODE, CLIMATE | LABORER (MAN) |
| Supervisor | FARMER | JOB CAPTAIN |
| Process | FROM MATTER TO LIFE | FROM LIFE TO MATTER |

On one side a few bags of seeds produce truckloads of
foodstuffs. On the other, toiling people, the laborers, produce truckloads of hardware.

Though the parallel is unfair because incomplete (the
hardware is supposedly an instrument for etherealization),
it points out the necessity of not only making the hardware well but making it only if essentially good, ontologically speaking. Thus, if the hardwares become ends in
themselves, the vectoriality of the process of matter-spirit
would be contradicted. In this light, manufacturing goods
might literally resolve itself into manufacturing evils. In
agriculture—this etherealizing assembly line—evil can only
be marginal, if at all conceivable (tobacco, opium . . .).

What of the supervisor of the assembly line, the farmer
himself and his family? Is the environmental condition in

which he is a condition favorable to etherealization? I think not.

The farm environment, even in a less forbidding climate, is not a cultural environment; that is to say, it is an environment deprived of those aspects that are specifically human inventions—the social and cultural intercourses and the richness of choices, options and learning they afford to the participant. Nor can the "electronic city" by itself furnish but pale substitutes for the corporality of environmental learning and experiencing the (good) city offers. The existential loneliness of life is almost fatally ingrained into existence of the tenuous farming community and the climate is not of any help.

## 2. *The City*

There are three kinds of forces that can make man behave respectfully toward his environment: 1) coercion; 2) self-interest; 3) reverence for life. Each of these has its own imperative.

For most of us the coercive way appears undesirable and even unrealistic. For most of us, the reverential way appears utopian and even sterile. It is, in fact, the only realistic way; the only truly etherealizing way. The ecological debacle we are in should tell us so.

*COERCION* Physically, coercion can produce good results. But those are skin deep and are at the expense of man's soul. Naturally, coercion has endless camouflages to work with—economic incentive being but one, and not by any means only or always the case. In coercion the imperative is not from the inner but from the outer and the results are in function of possible punishment. It is therefore the master imperative.

*SELF-INTEREST* Self-interest overlaps with coercion in the area where self-interest means survival. But it goes far beyond survival in at least two aspects. The driving force is internal not external. The extent of its efficacy is in function with the person's knowledge and "ancestry." In

*Performance is to creation what structure is to form. When one performs, one produces. When one creates, one becomes.*

making one responsible for one's own acts by the self-centeredness of the ego, self-interest extends its action up to the physical boundaries of one's possessions. Only a "broadminded" ego can connect his own well-being with that of others and consequently extend his respect for the environment beyond the one in exclusive control of his will. But no matter how fine might be the tuning of the ego, if his aim is and remains motivated by an inner impulse that sees in the outer world only something to control but not to partake in, the respect for the environment will be economic good sense but not much more. The imperative is, "Be your own master and make the environment show it."

*REVERENCE FOR LIFE* Reverence for life is a far more complex incentive toward a coherence of one's self with the outer self. It is the only incentive that can prevent one from falling prey to greed or gluttony and at the same time show as a result the real, fine tuning of the life of man to the existing universe. It is a teleological imperative fully adequate for the journey into creation-etherealization.

The person acting in self-interest will not let things "go to pot," inasmuch as he identifies with them in terms of economy and status. He cares about the market value of his holdings. If this achieves the goal of a good maintenance, it also entails all the limitation and grossness of the territorial imperative. It is exclusive instead of being inclusive; it keeps out the whole instead of being of it. As a general condition it negates the existence of the whole (dormitory suburbia). It is thus atomistic, grandular, insular: it is expedient. It is in fact non-congruent with what surrounds it. Furthermore, "My house is my castle," is a functional system when in use; it is a burden when it is only contractual or legal but not functional (not made use of).

The reverential relationship is not a legal-contractual

relationship, but an organic, existential one and the order it fosters is the order of the whole inasmuch as knowledge permits it. It is an effective interaction and a willful co-operation. It overflows boundaries of space and time: it is evolutionary.

The city must count on and permeate itself with this third kind of environmental respect in which the concept of ownership itself is etherealized and becomes the ownership of the mind: we own what we know and what we know is inseparable from the self. For the city to be more than just a clever enclave for action it has to be a lovable environment, capable of inspiring reverence.

One of the neccessary ingredients generating the reverential relationship is the conviction on the part of the citizenry that there is more to life than the economic solvency of society. *Homo economicus* is justified by *Homo sapiens* and not vice versa. In other words, the urban milieu must become an intensly cultural milieu because that is where the economic means find their own justification and man finds fulfillment. One can reverse the slogan, "Cultivate your learning so as to be successful," and say, "Your 'success' will lead you into learning or will lead you into nothing at all." By "learning" is meant here the sensitization of one's consciousness and the access to the creative universe, the universe of *Homo sapiens*.

If we try to bridge across the two frameworks—the one of the farmer and the one of the city dweller, both seeing man transcending matter—and try to come down to earth in search of the right instrument, on an earth whose climate is forbidding for months on end, we land realistically and pragmatically in the arcological milieu. There, the Canadian farmer, the etherealizer of stone, earth and light, and the Canadian urbanite, reverentially aware of what contains and sustains him, find the instrument and the devices for the development of their lives.

If this milieu is missing the farmer will see his life

stunted by isolation, cultural deprivation and hibernation. The city dweller will go on not realizing that what he is missing is almost all of what he unconsciously seeks: a friendly, blossoming urban life, not coerced into fringe performance by an obsolete layout, the slavery or bad logistics, the squalor of *laissez faire*, the economic imperative, and the inclemency of the climate.

This milieu is the arcological cityscape, pulled together, self-contained, acclimatized, alive with people going about the "business" of living, learning, producing, worshipping, creating, performing, throughout the year on the edge of the endless land upon which the seasons play their awesome and often inhuman cycle.

The American continent is very much in the hands of a society that has made self-interest into a fetish. The holy ground cannot be questioned without incurring the anathema of capitalism and *laissez faire*. Things are bad enough now to show the myopia and the utopias of the American pragmatism. It is the pragmatism of practicality not the pragmatism of reality. As the state of affairs is so poor if not so bad, it would be all the more important and regenerative if half of the continent, the Canadian half, would lessen its pride for the practical and would move away from the "American Dream," toward a reverential and real relationship with the earth. The American way is overpowering and spellbinding. It can be dealt with only if a far more powerful ideal sustains the soul of the people making up the Canadian society.

Upon surveying the alternatives, which cannot really be found in political manipulation, even those of the highest order, it seems that the true avenue is the reverential one, always personal and collective in one. Nor is this the avenue of the meek and the pious but the difficult and rigorous road of true compassion. By it, the challenge of nature, of technology, of a complex and troubled society, can and in time must be responded to, and the response,

Greed, bigotry, fear and the mysticism of the machine are the great pollutants. Greed sanctifies hoarding of "goods." Bigotry sanctifies the hatred for others' beliefs and edifies the (Pentagonal) war machines.

Fear reconfirms the holiness of hoarding and the "preparedness" for death. The mysticism of the machine is the awe toward the sorcery of production for the sake of filling the vacuums of fear and boredom surrounding lonely man. The fear of naught is made of countless faces. It could well be that the great lesson the red man offered to Western man was his ability to face naught: the strength he found in himself to accept the bleak loneliness of isolation.

if it is to be congruent with the past and with the evolutionary thrust cannot but be toward etherealization, away from materialism. Etherealization is to be supported by the best instrumentalities we can afford. Instruments can only be effectively found in the urban context. The state of the "urban art" must then be lifted from the desolate landscape of greed into the human dimension of grace—a "functioning," "delivering," "performing," living grace. A most difficult and most exhilarating task.

*Statistically is fatally, regardless of what level the statistician has reached—the gravitational level or the Medicare level.*

*Individually is willfully (destined). The destined finds matter to ponder, use, and sustain itself within the fatal as the fish does in the fluid sea. The fish finds life in the water; the water fruition in the fish.*

*No statistician, even the most omniscient, could have extrapolated man and all the other species from the preorganic world for the simple reason that the nature of the statistical is foreign to the nature of the creative.*

# SIMULATION AND BECOMING

The future and its predictability are a great concern of man. For a deterministic universe the predictability of the future is a function of knowledge. We have been able to predict cosmological patterns for thousands of years. What can we do when prediction is for non-deterministic phenomenology? Which is the more predictable: a moon trip by a robot or a day in the life of a man? Unhesitatingly, the trip to the moon. Keeping in mind that deficiencies in the system are consequences of unpredictable man's behavior or ignorance, we can see that the cause-effect sequence on the moon trip is all there for the taking. The trip is made before the trip is consumed. We call it "simulation." The difference between astronomical time and duration might be the key to the degree of usefulness of simulation. For an event in which deployment is only dependent on aspects of frequency and finite measurement, prediction is feasible (whenever the knowledge of digits is there). In this case, time is only relatively a future maker. Indeed, it could be that past, present and fu-

*The nature of the biological is the transcendence of the effect for each given cause. In this manner the future is really that which is utterly inconceivable because utterly nonexistent.*

*Technology is a "disjointed" phenomenon that single minds or minds teamed together go on developing in isolation or indifference toward the "rest," or better, in a "we will show them" frame of mind. How much their being instrument-minded makes them instrument-branded is of much concern.*

ture are only inventions of life and nonsensical for the mineral world. The radioactive decay is all "planned in an ever-present pattern measured by a beat we call 'time.'"

Time becomes a future maker when it becomes durational, that is to say, when it is a biophysical event. For an event in which deployment is dependent on biophysical sequences (duration), prediction becomes a guessing game because it really deals with the invention and not the discovery of the future. Determinism is hopelessly outmaneuvered by the unexpected, probability, by the improbable. And this is because the durational time is eminently—inventively and creatively—a future maker. It is the becoming into the naught of a real and incommensurable future.

One can see as a general rule that in any feasibility study the usefulness of simulation decreases in direct proportion to the increasing importance of duration, at the expense of time (your future between now and tomorrow and a moon shot).

Simulation, the instrument for prediction, is a splendid procedure, immensely useful in the universe of science-technology. Simulation is a poor procedure in the anticipation of becoming. It can become a deadly weapon, butchering the software of reality we call "life" when applied to the prediction of human events. The reason is simple. The cause-effect rule is not that "dogmatic" in the universe of mind and emotion, sociality and culture, work and leisure, learning and creating . . . the universe of man.

It is not that relevant for a more fundamental reason than that of the problem being too complex for programming, but possibly because the reality of life is ultra-rational and ultra-logical as it is evidently ultra-just and ultra-instrumental.

The yes-no of the computer is then not merely as sophisticated as a rusty nail used in a brain operation,

We are a self-governing, non-statistical micro-universe, fed by and oppressed by the statistician of the cosmos, "whom" is not a person, not a mind, not an ethic, but simply a "presence," a presence drifting in its particles as in its aggregation, in the direction of indifference.

Though the fatal has long ceased to be the only master of the animal, his destiny is still and only pursued in the non-personal body of the species. He moves through history (natural history) as within an impressive flood of willful matter exuding sweat, playfulness, tears and blood.

but as inadequate as the ruling of a slot machine on the love affair between two sentient beings.

Is simulation then to be a useless tool in the field of urban research? Certainly not, but its limitations are not marginal. They are limitations inherent to its nature. Its acrobatic magic does not, ever, resolve itself in the dance life is. And if this is not constantly reminded to the programmer, the risks are not worth the services. This has naturally wider implications than just limiting the area of competence of the computer. It strongly suggests that the skills necessary for the decision making are, in the field of urban planning, not of the purely rational kind, as those, for instance, applicable to a metallurgical or chemical process. Sure, we say, those are not human problems as the problems of the city are, and then, verbally rid of the equivocation, back we fall in our un-rational "rationalization."

The fact is that the rationalizing faculty is impotent in limiting its own meddling. As we cannot ask the circle to stop its circularity, so it is not possible to ask the intellect to explain to itself that the limits put to itself are still not rational limits.

The only thing that can stop silent the mind and can break the circle is a force or a pressure stronger than the mind itself.

In the sub-human world, the true rationalizing device is called "instinct." Instinct makes the animal do the right thing whenever the situation has a familiar aspect (cause-effect), not in the sense of being one of the things happening routinely in the life span of the animal, but routinely in the life span of the species. The rabbit as a species has been doomed to endless death by the fangs of the predator. When faced by the oncoming car, the rabbit is not helped by instinct. In fact, instinct will be more than often his undoer (rationalization in the case of man). The rabbit, in the presence of the oncoming car,

*. . . As in the infinitely large is the same randomness as it is in the infinitely small, a randomness that directs itself statistically; as if corpuscularity and immensity one because of nakedness, the other because of surfeit, would not disengage themselves from the tedium of non-expectation, so it seemed that in the finitude of the organism itself is the seat of non-randomness, the seat of willfulness.*

*Every time we make a rule out of a statistic, the future is taxed by this indifference in as much as it relies on a mechanistic determinism of the present and by the information mechanistically tabulated from a past in itself considered the fatal offspring of an ever greater mechanical remoteness.*

applies the same technique he successfully applies in the presence of the coyote or the falcon. He runs in short, sharply broken jogs. Very often one of those runs will put him under the car wheels since he unknowingly puts himself under a statistical law, a law which is less life saving than it is right to expect in the genetically familiar occasion. The rabbit has no resort to a trans-instinct that will improve his chances (ultra-rational for man).

His rationalization, instinct, cannot take up the challenge. He fails and has to accept passively the fate assigned to him by the laws of probability.

In man, as always, things are less clear-cut. As instinct is powerfully supplemented by reason, it becomes more obscurely active and, more than often, the non-rational decisions of instinct make of it the culprit of sorrow. Instinct, reason, trans-reason. Where and in what order must they work? At least three envelopes have slowly encircled the instinctual: the reflective envelope, the social envelope, and the cultural envelope. Knowledge, including self-knowledge, has constructed around the instinctual sphere a sizable structure of information that tends to depend less on the instinctual drives the greater the distance is which separates this knowledge from the instinctual sphere, and to depend more on the acquired ability of reflection, sociality and culture. This larger sphere is less and less genetic and more and more cultural. It is acquired, that is to say, it comes to the individual after the individual is genetically formed. It is the personal, social and cultural second nature of man. But if for man the instinctual is sub-rational, the personal, social and cultural are ultra-rational. Rationalization cannot cope with the first inasmuch as the automatic triggers of the instinctual behaviors are far swifter than the one-at-a-time operation of rationalization (the rabbit would be a sitting duck if he had to plan his escape). Does

*Time will stop beating when all the energies have slumbered down to the bottom of evenness. To keep its beat, turmoil must be fostered. Life, general and individual, pushes back further and further in the hole of time, the slowed-down beat of time itself, entropic time grinding to a halt as duration invades space.*

*If obsolescence takes the place of aging, time replaces duration; that is to say, the fatal prevails on the destined (willful). An environment which is simply a recharged mechanism is fatal in as much as it is obsolescent. Such a fatal environment will tend to destroy its opposite, life which is durational.*

rationalization, on the other hand, have what it takes to deal with the personal, the social, the cultural? That is to ask, in short, is simulation in such a case a legitimate instrument for planning? At first sight, one could say yes. The personal, social, and cultural are modular components per se logically definable. But even so (even if this were so) the same modular components go into structures whose individual organisms are hardly comparable. Not only do the structures differ, but the component bricks themselves are only germane to each other.

For two people standing side by side, the witnessing, acknowledgment and understanding of the same identical event is always different, at times antithetical . . . the torture of her child by the Nazi robot is an apocalyptic event for the mother, a routine to get over with for the desensitized man.

The fact is that people never, never stand side by side identical to one another. The longer the history of their past, the richer its content and the further apart they stand, utterly original, even in their most monstrous ways. Furthermore, day in, day out, the same original person swifts his originality on unpredictable pendulums. Then the rational way to rationally handle simulation would be to simulate each day, each moment of each person by an endlessly meticulous investigation of his past, his genetic make-up, his emotions and health conditions, etc., ad infinitum, then simulate the interaction of this mountainous package, abstract of a life, with the other thousands of identically mountainous packages no less abstract. The conclusion is that the only rational simulation of life is the living of life itself. Duration is, by definition, a non-simulatable phenomenology. That is, simulation is strictly irrational when applied to the ultra-rational phenomenon that life is.

Indeed, simulation is for process. It is not for becoming. Process is, as observed before, an event measured by

*Man's world is the world of non-randomness. To have it controlled by statisticians is to betray its nature and the species of man with it. Statistics are nothing more than the envelope of data wrapped around the unraveled substance of becoming.*

*The "reflective time" is duration that, imprisoned by the fatal beat of material time and conditioned by the acceleration or deceleration of biological time finds its own reality in its power to densify or dilute the action of the mind and by so doing free man from the cage of the fatal (time).*

frequence. It is, at its best, untied from the idiosyncrasies of man (automation) and efficiency is its credo. It is a metronomic sequence working on atomic time disregarding duration, the bio-psychic beat of life (the automatic assembly line can be made to go at different speeds). Process is that portion of reality that instrumentalizes the other portion, the living and the ontological portion to which instrumentality is subservient. The stove, the pots and pans are instrumental to the making of a good dish. The good dish partakes more directly of the metaphysical world than the stove and the other tools do. The metaphysical world comes in full bloom in the presence of the table and the company dining together. Shade by shade reality can be sorted out and logically displayed from the extreme of pure instrumentality to the other extreme of pure spirit. Roughly speaking, process belongs to the first half; becoming, to the second. One is the world of cause-effect, simulable, the deterministic world. The other is of the improbably, unpredictable, unsimulable world. What then is the instrument that is up to the task of "planning" the environment for man? It is none other than the exceptional person who has found in himself the intensity and the drive to be a speaker and a conceiver for the common man. He is the man in possession of a trans-instinct.

One could call him an instinctualized intellect that can bridge from the sub-rational to the ultra-rational and land in the eye of the human reality itself. This should not, as it does, upset the "common" man. Isn't he agreeable to the notion that the Einsteins and the Picassos are rare specimens and isn't planning for an intensely human environment a most difficult task demanding rare insights?

If we give in to the idea that a good team of programmers will come up with the most reliable job, we are in for, at best, a bland, utterly demythologized solution. I use the term "mythology" purposely. We think

*On the entropic incline, the willful constructs the terraces of the living. Plants and animals root themselves in the sound soil of the statistical (predictable) and go on locally defying and defeating it.*

that myth and metaphysics are burdens on man's back. We push aside the old myths with an utterly mythical rationale that mysticizes technology and change, as if they meant anything at all deprived of the forces that have originated them, forces that are, as far as it can be conjectured, the only reasons for their existence. Myth and comfort cannot coexist, as myth is a specifically uncomfortable but creative stance of man vis-à-vis the mystery of the universe. Our trouble is not that we live too much by myth, but rather that our myths are shallow, cluttered by the pollutants of our affluent-opulent utopia.

The instrument is because the mind has willed it, but the instrument is not the offspring of the mind. It is purely a device the mind makes to create better offsprings. The instrument cannot order nor speculate nor project what the next move of the mind is any more than the paws of the tiger can modify the iron sway of instinct that will make the tiger be on the run after the prey.

Only the long stay of instrumentality among the human environment will mark the mind. It will mark the mind; it will not make it, as no discrete thing can make a non-discrete thing. Between them is, in this case, the blazing fire of compassion. Thus, free will becomes a concrete entity handling the instruments of its invention. The aim of this free agent is not limited to invention of instruments as this is the prerogative of biological life. It is instead, and beyond, the creation of a new, unpredictable non-simulable reality.

# ESTHETICISM AND ESTHETOGENESIS

The esthetic world began as the intermediary between the earthly and the otherworldly, an intermediary for defenseless and mortal man whose skin contained all that took to make him be, whose outer was all that he could take from for survival and becoming, and all that could crush him by brutal blows or by subtle insinuations and penetration into its being. The esthetic was then a work of anguish and hope, of atonement and thanks, of defiance. It was the beginning of an esthetogenesis; at first, the genesis of a universe that would make bearable to man the fate of his inception, then a universe made by man where man would be a free agent. To the world, this esthetic universe would be the intrusion of man's demands and the infusion within the black and dumb universe of the light and sound of logos. When hedonism infiltrated the sacred grounds, esthetogenesis grew a parasite. The lessening of the tension at the edge of survival gave the parasite food for development. Only the best filters—artists—have throughout history kept the tree of esthetogenesis alive and growing. For the rest, it was a question of having one finger into the action, regardless of how pertinent the participation was.

Today, presumptively free from fear and doom, esthetic man is one with extravagant man. Hedonism-estheticism has taken over with a twist. The technological demon has had not too much to do to tempt and to corrupt the "artist." If only the Fausts of our museums would go and have firsthand experience with the enclaves of the technological Mephistopheles, they would see how cheap they themselves come and how poorly they are regarded by their masters. Indeed, the anguish and the terror and hope and defiance and atonement are in the technological enclaves and not in the studio of the artist. The artist is a shriveled figure chained to his estheticism, ingrown and often septic.

There, where the incredible megamachine of technology grinds out steel and plastics, concepts and inventions, electronic and chemical brains, bombs and rockets, there is where the anguish of the species desperately and quasi-hopelessly seeks a catharsis.

The artist has reduced his task to put-ons and whimpers, an abysmal fall from the exaltation of being one in a trinity, the mediator between the human and the ultra-human. But those creators were limitlessly ambitious men, as the founders of religions were. There was no limit as to why their search was at the core of reality, and how and where it would operate and evolve would not be of prime concern. Were they not creators of a third world, the world of compassionate beauty?

The game player, the toy maker, the usurper of the arts, the jester and paranoiac, the opportunists and their court of joiners can have none of this. The anguish of man is captive of the technocratic resolve of not letting any discovery lie idle, nor any bit of cunning or cleverness go lost to the sorcery of his tools. Man himself is captive as

### PROCESS AND GROWTH

*Process is "manipulation" by outer decision.*
*Process belongs to the technological.*
*Growth is "manipulation" by inner decision.*
*Growth belongs to the bio-mental.*

*Process is a performance of technology which acts by way of oversimplification.*
*Growth is a performance of the bio-mental which acts by way of complexification.*

*Process defines changes.*
*Growth defines engrossment.*

*Contemporary man is mesmerized by change and is starved by lack of engrossment.*

the process has displaced the becoming, the hows are crushing the whys.

Process is the producer of change, but this is only half of the story, and not the most important, the instrumental half. I see change as of two kinds. The first kind is the change brought about by what I call "process." Process is the transformation of the inanimate world, the mineral and the technological world. Process is really timeless in the sense that it operates more on frequencies than time lapses. (One can accelerate or decelerate a process.) The most crucial character of process is that it is reversible (even though limitations of know-how might prevent it). Determinism governs process. The second kind of change is that brought about by what I call becoming. Becoming is irreversible and qualifies and is qualified by duration, the bio-psychological time by whose beats life develops. Creativeness is the etherealizing aspect of becoming.

We have made the barbarous mistake of identifying process with becoming. The confusion is killing us and civilization. The production-consumption carnival has put process on the altar. Process, not becoming, is the business of business and the business of the ecological debacle. Becoming, on the other hand, is incapable of destruction, inasmuch as becoming is the antithesis of un-becoming. The opulent society is unbecoming.

Duration-complexity belongs to becoming. Frequency-process tends toward complicatedness. An organism is duration-complexity oriented. A machine is frequency-complicatedness oriented. Our present society is still mechanico-complicated. It must metamorphose toward the durational-complex. It is only in the esthetic phenomenon, the esthetogenesis of things, that process and becoming can come into fusion. There is where life must tend toward, to make full use of the energetic universe without itself being distracted from the tide of evolution and into a mechano-deterministic event, durationally indifferent, that is to say, reversible, ethically nil.

*Creativeness is the great body in whose shadow gregariousness can perform. It is utterly cruel, because misleading, to propose five to seven billion creators. Most of us create by proxy (mimesis). It is then right to say that the human species is creative and illusory to make of creativity a blanket event. The creation (estheto-compassionate event) is not an electric blanket, but a blazing flame too hot to be handled indiscriminately. It is the other sun, the non-deterministic sun of becoming.*

What then of the arts? They hardly are a part of life, as they cannot be any longer the intermediary between the mortal and the "immortal." It might well be for the better. The esthetic world has always been far more than an interpreter or a soother between two irreconcilable worlds. By its fall the esthetic man sees his tasks endangered but at the same time clarified. The esthetic is the third world, synthesis and etherealization of both the other two. When it is not that, when it does not perform, it is automatically absent. An instrument can perform poorly and still be an instrument. A poor poem is simply not an esthetic event. It is a miscarriage of knowledge and emotions that adds no novelty to the flow of becoming. It is not a creation. So it is not that the art can be on top or on the bottom or in between the phenomenon of man. It can only be as its synthesis (utter economy) or it is not.

I then call museums those storehouses where smothering the few and far apart esthetogenetic strands is a swollen congeries of personalized fragments of matter for which both the materials and the process carry the burden of a lonely and puny revolt, none of an altogether more compassionate if minute self-originating conception; this is not the great age of esthetogenesis.

Man is a prisoner as never before of the sorcery feasibility has shrouded him with. The acceleration of change, of which process is the procurer, presents confounded man with today's icon that has made obsolete yesterday's icon. The icon being the corporate image, the engineering feat, the car, the SST, the multiple warhead, the rock hit, etc. The last icon of all, man himself, swept along to the waste heaps where obsolescence nests and seeps back into matter-energy.

And as the artist has all but given up, the technocrat at the lower floor carries on the burden he is not structured to carry. Indeed, the anguish cannot but grow, the loneliness becomes more steely as more and more matter is forged into servicing a shrinking ethos and a collapsing hierarchy of gods (gross national product, etc.).

Esthetogenesis is not a rescue ship and, misused as that, it will not break the deterministic lock technocracy is snapping on man. Religion and philosophy are the lockbreakers. For the real esthetic man, the task is to transfigure the deterministic universe, in all its crystalline logic and rationality, into a compassionate, ultra-logical and ultra-rational reality.

# MAN AND SEPARATENESS

The death of Martin Luther King denounced again the evil of racism. It would do well to his sacrifice if we brought the very fact of racism into a larger container, the house of separateness. In it the question is given a dimension of envelope, the sphere and the sanction of the homosphere of the earth. Race segregation is the focusing of destructiveness on the most tender tissue of such envelope, the person. But it is not what separateness is in the total context of life. In such context, separateness is the breaking of the process of learning and performance in two major fragments, analysis and synthesis, and the discarding of the second.

It is not really poor communication that is responsible for evil but poor understanding. (Note then the importance of environmental information vis-à-vis canned information.) The process of investing oneself into the real is always begun with a cleaver or a clumsy analysis of the available information. Young or old, cultivated or ignorant, we collect information in an analytical frame of being. If we find time as collectors of data, we are reluctant to pause and let time (organic time) impregnate the information bits with the cement of synthesis. We glue such fragments on the billboards of the brain and return to them in need, to single out the black or the white with no context to them and in a thick haze of abstraction.

## UNDERSTANDING

What practically happens is that we constantly broadcast as much as we receive and what comes in goes out, as if bounced by a mirror, bits incoming, bits outgoing, undigested, unintegrated, segregated. But the value of information is that—once taken in as a building material—it is used, one of the many, in the construction of a structure, the structure of one's own life congruent to the larger structure of society and the structure of the world.

The key word is congruence. Separateness is where congruence is not. Congruence is where separateness has been canceled. Life should be the use of reality in such a way as to wear out the threads of the nets imprisoning things to the point where this net of separateness is consumed away and things, individual but free, can reach and touch each other.

## PASSIVITY

If we behave as simple reflectors, we do not participate, that is to say, we are not decision makers. We sway as the current of events moves. For a universal condition of passivity, the current of events is made up of the collective swaying of all the reflectors. And always somewhere, someone or something has his hand on the throttle and commands, sways and counter-sways. His power of control is in the fragmentation of the controlled in which the controlled, analytical and unco-ordinated mosaic is not moved nor moving toward a synthesis that collectivizes every single stone to form a context of consequence. If such a synthesis had occurred, the single bits would have been related, made to make friends with other bits already transferred into the single whole of which they are part and parcel, within the folds of the mind.

If so, then at emission time such emission would not be the inordinate reflection of fragments of information but a conscious and willful response to the outer proposition.

## MENTAL SEGREGATION

When I hear "nigger" and I shout back "nigger," I am a dull, if polished, fragment of matter. When I read that a Black neighbor equals depreciation of real estate and I bark it out to the four winds, I am again a dull pebble. I have failed to integrate the packaged information within reality. I simply cast it within the fragment, the practical fragment of such reality. In so doing I buy a little time for myself and make of my future a nightmare, the one this nation is in now.

The shadow-reality of a real estate value is clearly denounced by the precariousness of the conscience that must go in defending it, the separateness, from the swelling of a whole biological phenomenon groping for a cosmic component, of the barricaded anguish, in individuals conditioned by long years of passive, mirror-like behavior. True pragmatism has no hesitation in rejecting the shadow-reality of many of the acts caged on the altar of the practical. A burning city is not practical to anyone, least of all to insurance companies. But we have institutionalized it and made it part of our own reality. The fire bomb and the throwing hand are only incidental. Arsonism is in the separateness we nurse with determinate and irrational care.

In the fine-arts world the universality of the personal expression would be the same groping for a wholeness of intents, if not of results. The artist is not a reflector, as is often said, but an integrator possessed by an extrapolative faculty that permits him to do more than others with the same amount of analytical input, so much so that sometimes he even creates.

## SYNTHESIS

The power of synthesis can and must be cultivated. There is very little significance in any initiative that fails to point at the indisputable convergence of even the most "unrelated" performances. The esthetic performance is essentially synthetic and, as all synthesis, is a centration of energies. In esthetics the incommensurability between the limited physical and energetic bulk gone in the composition of the esthetic object is clear; let us say the incommensurability between a painting and the hold that it has on the soul of man. The sur-energy of the esthetic object is the measurement of its own substance. This sur-energy is of synthetic nature. It is the packaging or miniaturizing of powers ordinarily tenuous because scattered into low-tensed, physico-temporal areas yielding low or nil usefulness. The esthetic object is a center of radiation around which man congregates singly or collectively to be participatory or witness to an act of creation. It is crucial to emphasize that a scanty soul has not the energetic reservoir for the compression of inputs into wholes, wholes whose outpourings of radiance are the esthetic object.

To cultivate one's soul is then the quest that will back up the skills of the eyes, the ears, the hands and the body with the synthetic power of the mind and ultimately will cast aside the cages of separateness. Separateness is a peculiar invention of man and it is a menace to his position within the evolving universe. Small or large, the individual work is a contribution toward or an inquiry on the body of the species. The responsibility is personal and awesome and the punishment is as intrinsic to the performance as much as are the rewards. Each of us is a universal man or woman because we all are of the universe. To neglect this is purely to neglect oneself, a neglect that kills.

*To achieve paradise is for the robot and its congested mind. For man paradise is behind and lost, and justly so, as infantile longings are futile exercises. But the futile exercise of billions of minds can well do the species in as savagely and hideously as any extra-human force can.*

# PSYCHOSOMATIC MAN (Psychology and Environment)

What makes for a psychological common ground between two or more individuals does not happen in a physical vacuum; it is an event contained and conditioned by the environment. In fact, the psychosomatic immanence is a momentous outcome of environmental conditionings (survival of the fittest, for one), co-present to and formative of the evolution of soma and psyche.

To maintain that psychological man is separate or more important than environmental (somatic) man is non-sensical, as it considers man as nothing more than an abstraction of his mind. Psychological man is the offspring of somatic man as "social psyche" is the offspring of social soma, the characterization of the biological society by the environmental (physical) pressures.

The distrust, borne by a too easily disillusioned youth, for anything that stands between two souls or between a multitude of them (Woodstock) has had the negative effect of making a desert for somatic man in which sterility the psyche will supposedly blossom.

Who but the mad and the dead would be willing to give up as of this moment the access (for man) to the written universe, to the music of man, to the world of his mind which he has physically constructed, to the institution itself of civilization on the presumption that after all what counts is the direct relationship between what at such a degree of deprivation would be not more than two or more naked apes?

## CONTAINER AND CONTENT

If the spirit is an offspring of matter (the only one), and not vice versa, psychological man is the offspring of somatic (physiological) man. For the same logical congruence the psychological media of society can only make itself as if spinning into being by the fertility of the physical environment. It is the irreversibility of the process of tangibility into intangibility that demands the precedence of the container so as to energize the content. If we do not dam the running water, we will not be able to make use of the potential energy, energy of position, of environment, of the water. The "free water" will go for a so-called natural balance of things. That same balance of things which has been disrupted by all, none excluded, doings of man. A "natural balance" which accepts life only up to threshold of consciousness, as beyond it willfulness and not naturalness is in (partial) command. The simplest ecosystem is the mineral universe. It is the ecosystem of non-life. Should it be the measure of things? Beyond it the ecosystem is to a degree also a psycho-system as rudimentary as the psychic context might be, the psychology of a vegetable, for instance.

There is a factual prevalence, if not pre-eminence, of somatic man on psychic man. Somatic man has the ancestry of billions of years of biological life; psychic man, an ancestry measured by the few hundreds of thousands of years of *Homo erectus*. This pre-eminence makes mandatory the existence of a physical environment adequate to his "needs." One of those, and the one that more and more should prevail, is the psychological food that nurtures his spirit. But this food germinates in the environment and it is reinvested in it, as a matter of growth, by the manipulating forces of the same, and thus growing, spirit. Manipulation is a surcharging of matter with psychic tension which . . .

1. Disrupts the crystalline-statistical order of matter itself (and thus predisposes the staging of chaos).
2. Produces chaos itself as soon as the psycho-tension abandons the manipulated (man-made) object.

This is the littering of nature by man and his doing. The used-up napkin is discharged of the tension represented and incorporated in its potential use. Pre-use is potential charge. Post-use is inertial state. It can and must retain a charge, even if residual, in order to carry the closing of the "paper" cycle. The worn-out napkin is a dead napkin. The price tag of a used napkin symbolizes the residual charge. Its price tag is to be found in the whole ecological dividend for which an open cycle is a passive cycle. "In the red," as the saying goes. The greater the surcharge, the greater the potential for littering. The yard full of broken-down equipment and worn out tools is a powerful synopsis of such littering. The letdown from the surcharge (performance) is the causation of a brutish post-usefulness condition which, in a way, is even protocosmic for the absence in it of the statistical order governing the universe (as the used-up napkin to a far lesser degree does also). The world of litter and waste is the world where the spirit has departed and rationality of matter-energy was beforehand purposely warped for the sake of the now departed spirit.

In those yards of naught is where, by the way, the "artist" of today often finds his subject matter with the mythical illusion of using it only as a media for the expression

*Anything we make carries an open price tag and an undisclosed price tag. This last price is not less real by being ignored. In fact, by not appearing on the official balance sheets it becomes the decisive voice on the timetable for survival. Pollution is the most comprehensive sum of the undisclosed price tags, and pollution starts with the cigarette, the napkin, the water faucet running idle, the bric-a-brac, and ends with a biosphere graveyard . . . the price of irrelevance in the face of a phenomenon which is relevance: Life.*

of his soul. Such soul is often only as large as the media he is manipulating, an instance in which the message is nothing but a refurbished media. The object he therefore comes up with can find atonement only in contrast, irony or paradox, but none in grace, harmony, transcendence. Paradox, irony, contrast are proto-esthetic. They can only frame or synchronize, punctuate or sharpen, but cannot be themselves the stuff of the metamorphosis of matter into spirit at the rarefied level of creation.

Our cityscapes are, more than they should ever be allowed to be, like those yards full of broken-down equipment. In this case, broken-down homes sheltering breaking down human beings, families, societies. If the planner plays the "practical" game of refurbishing-remodeling, restoring, he must be aware that his "masterpiece" is somehow abortive. Who needs a masterpiece, it is said. Who needs less than that, I would reply. Do we hope for anything less than a masterpiece when we buy a car or a dinner? Isn't never getting it the alternative that creeps inside of us and slowly cripples the best which is there? There is an innate reverence in the way we step into situations expectantly and hopefully but to be soon turned off. This reverential expectation for things masterfully done, justly organized, coherently related to all the other masterfully done things. The psyche is then thwarted as the soma is constantly bruised by the arrogance of grossness and ugliness. It is the sensorial and sensitized animal that urges the psyche into withdrawal. Furthermore, the environment can kill physiological man or, correspondingly, it can cause both exhilaration and reverence in him.

The cruelty inflicted upon the "deprived" and the "derelict" is in the paradox and the existential absurdity of insisting that the psychic man can ignore somatic man, that man can really be not what pours into him through his senses after this subject matter has been re-elaborated and made self, but can be some ethereal stuff disjointed from matter and structure, texture and climate, marble or rotten wood, flowers or rats. Isn't there an intrinsic schizophrenia in the therapy that works on an imaginary man and does not pay attention to the man who has constantly to wage battle with his own animality, sensoriality, impressionability?

The chill of the soul is administered by the handyman of a brutal environment . . . the landlord, the cop, the pusher, the moneylender, the alcoholic, the mugger, the social worker . . . Unless the therapy is turned also and at the same time to such environment, the "insane" condition is there to stay. And yet, a sane condition will not be found in a Reston or a Columbia as those are not options congruent to the earthly condition but parasitic instances of an already unreasonably fractured style of life.

## THE PLANNER

Given the ambiguity and the complexity of the context, why should a person, the "planner," be entrusted with the responsibility of planning the physical environment?

1. If something has to happen, somebody must be the directional and driving force, not the computer or the depersonalized corporated entity.

2. Who, if not the individual most interested and "trained" on the subject matter of organization of physical structures and materials in usable patterns? He might not be the ideal impersonation of our needs but he might well be the least objectionable for the task.

3. The true scope of "architecture" (arcology) beside and beyond the sheltering of society is not the hosting of bio-physiological events but it is the setting up of the hotbed for the instauration of new physio-mental circumstances. This is, by the way, why it is hard to put human substance into a gas station or a laundromat. For those, the intangible coincides with naught.

4. The just observation that the architect-planner is not

sufficiently qualified does not cancel the fact that he is the most qualified yet. As it is for the inventor of the typewriter he must be sure that the machine can reproduce letters of the alphabet, not necessarily to know what kind of message will be typed—that is to say the tangible environment, not the events it will serve for. But since, as a participant in the psychosomatic event, he is also one of the information makers, this aspect of his work will shine through or will dull the total message. This is the intangible aspect and it is one of the rare instances where the media is also the message, that is to say, environment (the media) is the society (the message).

5. As technology is of diminishing capability (reliability) the more complex the demanded performance is, it is quite natural that in the definition of the environment of man a preponderant task is given to the trans-technological. The trans-technological becomes the common patrimony of man when it is at the same time personal, that is to say identifiable with his "author," and universal, that is to say of such a strength and vibrance that confers to it a universal "usefulness." The esthetic is the only category which fits the description.

By this long way round, I want to say finally that not only is the environment the flesh and blood of somatic man, but as somatic man is inseparable from psychological man, and the flesh and blood for him resides in the trans-technological, the end afforded by the means (technology), such environment cannot be only orderly and friendly, it must also be esthetic, transfigurative. Short of such quality the environment can at most be the neutral ground for a psychosomatic man deprived of its own nature.

*Our idea of an earth bled white, made by man into a squalid desert, a moon or Martian-scape is another of those romantic and presumptuous self-assertions. The ecology "sub-species evil man" will simply be a more mineral ecology and it will remain so with the self-extinction of the family of man.*

# BULLDOZER MAN (Earth Moving)

On the premises that what makes life possible on this planet is the existence of a few inches of topsoil on the geology which is not under water, one is to be aware of how good the reasons must be for scrapping, digging and altering the local balance. Soil destruction has been a historical determinant as much as the invention of farming. What the farmer may learn not to do may now be done by the land speculator and, in general, by twentieth-century "Bulldozer Man."

Then what the architect and landscape architect may do in their little enclaves is irrelevant or it would be irrelevant if not for the fact that what touches the land touches directly on public patrimony, no matter how clean are one's own paper titles to it. In this contest, free enterprise shows itself to be more than just inadequate. It is faulty, destructive and, in the full context of civilization, plainly evil.

To inquire into the hows of a process without having sound reasons for the validity of the process itself is as dangerous as to wage war because one has an army. How often this is done one needs no reminder.

I would say that most of the time our business should be the prevention of the soil from moving (see later) rather than moving it; somewhat of a secondary importance is the cunning we apply to the process and to the promotion of it. We overgraze with cattle and we "overgraze" with bulldozers. The hunger of the latter is awesome.

Earth moving not co-ordinated in the larger scheme of climate, sun, wind, rain and frost action, water sheds, soil composition, vegetation, animal life and social environment is not auspicable. Chances are that in time it will be a hindrance to the vitality of the area in question.

Earth moving is a large ecological undertaking. It is justifiable if the resulting ecology is "better" than the original one.

If altering the landscape is dangerous for the ecology of the land, and thus dangerous for man himself, burrowing our dwellings in the crust of the earth is a downright and direct mortification of life; an entombed civilization would probably be very efficient but also brutalizing.

The survival and evolution of the land species is the result of an unbelievable and triumphant struggle. By it beauty comes into things and, what is more important, beauty comes in the eyes of the beholder. The esthetic sense is the child of the sun, the air, the light, the wind, etc.; bury living man and you bury the reasons for his sensibility.

We must be aware that the utilitarian aspect of our senses will decline in importance in proportion to the subtlety of our technology. For instance, our safety is less and less dependent on good sight and a sharp sense of smell. In the near future our senses will work almost purely as esthetic windows opening on the outside of our physically confining skin.

For an antiseptic, conditioned, buffeted, sealed and fully man-made environment like the underground, we may find more usefulness in an invented and cheaply produced set of sensors to superimpose and supplant our biological sensory devices, whose structure speaks of poor objectivity.

Under such conditions man will shape himself into a sort of rounded cube, a bullion, partly flesh and partly an electro-magnetic field and post-transistors. He will be a sensitized bullion better equipped for the homogenized environment of the underground than for the vagaries of the sun, air, rain and wind.

To complete the forecast on bullion man, one may add that for a society of his kind information will be instantaneous and remote; thus, the scattering tendency of today, a small earth for each family, will reap its final reward: each individual bullion (sex a gross device of primitive man) will be buried deep in soil or rock in the manner toads are found in excavations. Then man shall have inherited the earth.

Things and organisms are very much confined processes. Why do we and nature encapsulate processes? We do so to reach an optimum of efficiency. The best capsule, insulating, airtight, strong, pressurizable, isothermic, stable and permanent is the underground. Thus, it seems unavoidable that any non-biological undertaking of a utilitarian and productive nature will sooner or later move its quarters under the surface of the earth.

Luck or providence or sheer timing makes mass production coincide, or quasi, with cybernation. Man does not have to follow his machine into the underground. He must not, not for reasons of efficiency nor for reasons of survival. He must find a better future than that.

A convergence of different elements presents us with a promising pattern, an implosive pattern:

1. The spatial coincidence of liveliness with the bio-psychic compactness, a direct consequence of the logistic of matter and information-communication.
2. The need for the preservation of a nature whose ecology is precariously balanced between what has been the fruition of about three billion years of history and the intrusion of homo faber, centered, one could say, on today's doings.
3. The use of cybernation setting instrumentality as an ever powerful platform from which man may be able to take flight in his search for sustained creativity (freedom).

The reading of the pattern is:

1. Man and society will cluster in high-density organisms that are fully three-dimensional. Such new cities, neonatural phenomena, will be architectural ecologies: arcologies, the landscape of reflective, complex and creative man.
2. Such man-made, "thick" ecologies will be surrounded by the open countryside, farm land, parks, prairies, deserts, wastelands, forests, mountains, seas (and space). The individual citizen, physically and constantly at the threshold between city and countryside, will have the best of both.

    It is a truism that land conservation is coincidental with the existence of beautiful, lovable cities.
3. The technological world of research, organization and production will sink into the bowels of the earth where pressure, vacuum, heat, cold, radiation and atmospheric sophistication are possible and efficient to the performance of the production cycles.
4. The introduction of the vertical dimension and the consequent organization of space and activities in totally

new frames and scale will open for sensible man unforeseeable horizons.

The relevance for earth moving is direct. Earth moving
will follow the same tenets of high concentration. For each
new city there will be a colossal program of excavation
and production of materials: sand, gravel, stone, cement,
lime, soil, etc. Such quarries and the drainage structure
of the whole system will suggest, case by case, the organization of a major park totally man-conceived and man-
made. Thus, the scar left by the excavating and processing
plants can be transformed into a focal element for the out-
door life of the citizen, for play, leisure, culture and sport.
The ingredients are geology, water, vegetation and the
awesome presence of the city.

The new cities will not crawl inside the earth, but their
roots will reach, by necessity, far into the geological back-
bones, and the excavated ground not transformed into
construction material will be used for the ground cityscape.

As a very general rule I would say that the amount of
earth moved should be proportional to the thickness of
the system to which it relates. Large rearrangements of
landscape, when not of an agricultural nature, are not
warranted by a veneer of one-story housing. The landscape that man is going to create will not be of a one-level
kind. Thus, the ground rearrangement will be ever more
concentrated and dependent on the conditions established by the scores of man-made grounds above it.

If it is true that the electric age is the organic age, then
the aggregation of man into the megalopolis of the mechanical age will articulate and super-aggregate itself in
organisms that, far from posing the obstacles to growth
and knowledge that blight today's cities, will be crucible
of new cultural patterns.

We constantly hammer on the concept of change.
Well, change is not really the physical ability to build and

destroy frenetically and at will, but the fluidity allowed
to life within the structures, the physical and mental structures that we build. Thus, built-in obsolescence and the
precariousness it carries may not indicate affluence and
redundancy, nor liveliness, but conceptual misery and environmental squalor.

Looking once more at the precariousness of life, dependent as it is on the topsoil of the land, one can say in a very
literal sense that the task of mechanized man is not one
of moving earth but of stopping the earth from moving,
bringing to a halt the flow of topsoil from the land's upper
belts down to the bottom of the seas. In the total ecological balance, the action of bulldozer man will be measured
by his ability to conserve more than by his ability to alter.

The realistic, not the practical, planning for a future
culture would start at the upper edges of the water
sheds with bulldozer man enthroned between coherence
and vision.

We could then teach a thing or two to statistical nature
and bring greatness and splendor to our society. It is as if
the grace of harmony should descend on the earth as the
"gravity of the mind" in the same way if not the same
compulsion by which water and soil must fall from the
above to the below. One could say that the investiture
of humaneness on the planet has to be gravitational to be
evolutive and implosive, moving toward the center, and I
would add nodular and ribbed.

Gravity is the number one ruler of our environment
as bulldozer man well knows. Thus, to start at the bottom
is literally to prepare one's own burial, and that may well
be what bullion man is after.

Now that we have the framework of a culture and the
power to build within it, we should pack and walk to the
top of the mountain and from there (forty days of fast-
ing?) firmly, awesomely and compassionately we should
unfold, descend and grow scores of incredible flowers, not

necessarily the flowers of evil, even though some of them may recall Babel towers and Noah's ark.

If bulldozer man has no use for such nonsense, it is because his literate or brain-leaden counterpart is fidgeting about matters of a practical nature and of an irrelevant reality.

Earth moving still retains the magic of timelessness. Where the earth is moved landscapes are produced and cast, but, if one's eyes may be fooled, the ecology will not.

The grossness of man's toil will be reflected in unexpected forms, from the most ephemeral to the most lasting, but seldom for the better. Yet, if there is a thing which affords man an eternity of a sort, that thing is the molding of the earth's surface. The forming of the earth together with bits of bone and pots are what is physically left of pre-history, a proto-bulldozer era. One hopes that the humanized landscape will well serve the purpose of man the creator, not man the speculator.

We have the whole thickness of the earth to handle and exploit. We have only the thin unstable skin of topsoil, and the seas, to procure for us the biological energies indispensable for life.

# THE SCULPTURE EARTH

An air museum should be established. It would be a modified jet plane so as to permit the best visibility of the land below. It would show the ordeal and the triumph of the spirit and the massive contribution of the farmer toward the esthetogenesis of the earth, a true transfiguration coextensive to the earth masses. The Montana-Calgary landscape is many thousand square miles of "abstract" concrete painting-sculpture in a constant process of change. It gives the lie and all but shatters the petty exercises of the earth sculptors and museum directors.

Life on earth is locked in the aggregate, a few inches deep, that the ancestry of life (life and man) has compounded. Topsoil cannot be manufactured or imported. It is instead dumped into the seas at rates carelessly boosted by man in quest for immediate reward. A topsoil bank is as essential to us as any other undertaking viewing things beyond the day at hand. In the global perspective, because of the quasi-unlimited capability for action and makeshift of man, land and water conservation are

*Duration-complexity belongs to becoming. Frequency-process tends toward complicatedness. An organism is duration-complexity orientated. A machine is frequency-complicatedness orientated. Our present society is still mechanico-complicated. It must metamorphose toward the durational-complex.*

the fundamentals to observe in earth sculpture. The by-passing of such conditions by bio-chemistry and technology is not in view, the main reason being possibly that duration (time-growth) is a parameter as yet uncontrollable by man. This organically unshrinkable beat of time is the one and the same that the artistic act alone can abridge without pre-empting it; making it more intense instead. Art thus considered, the pulling together of past and future out of the grindstone of time through a particular action, becomes the trust that man applies on the environment to construct his own nature: the making of an environment in harmony with the living man. One could then say that by the esthetic action, and respectful of the bio-physical rules of water and soil conservation among the many others, we can act upon nature with an impact measuring up to nature itself. The result is an integration of the physical and the metaphysical.

Actually, man intervenes in the natural cycle in two main ways:

1. By faking the lawful casualness of nature with an unwarranted casualness of his own, as one who now and then is reminded by an ache to take care of some physiological function. The apparent lack of rules in nature is, in fact, the resultant of an infinite number of them complementing and interacting with each other. Thus, the pattern nature conforms to when not touched by man is the expression of this resultant: beyond casualness is the unremitting guidance of self-making laws.

2. By establishing one or many arbitrary orders useful to him at a specific historic moment: the productive, the functional, the defensive, the esthetic, the playful orders. Any of those will be an oversimplification of nature's order and, as such, constantly precarious. In both instances, man is bound to disrupt, more or less

drastically, the existing balance, an altogether dangerous and essential element fostering life. The disruption
may be called: positive, when by its appearance latent
energies are awakened, energies which will carry on a
new cycle; negative, if paralysis is set in, by which what
was is destroyed and the present does not foretell of
anything with which to fill the future.

## POWER WITHOUT WISDOM

The extreme of the first instance would see the return of
the primitive societies of food gatherers and hunters, with
spare and irregular use of the fruit of the earth (grasses,
grains, fruits, and vegetables). The extreme of the second
instance could be symbolized by the Italian garden of the
sixteenth–seventeenth centuries, where man imposes rigidly his own rules (esthetic) on the extant ground. What
is singular in our present position is that on one hand we
have acquired the material power to remake things in our
own image. On the other hand, we lack the fortitude
and the fundamentals to do so spiritedly. We do not
know what our image is. We are hence casual and brutal
in one and the same.

Man may well come out of the earth, into the un-
differentiated Hades of post-life, or he may face nature as
it is and transfigure it as he believes. Wisdom may belong
to either one. Man (Western man) belongs to the latter.
If man is only the most active tool of earthly nature for
concealed ends, then he and the beaver belong together.
If man is to transcend earthly nature for even more concealed ends, then it is up to him to mold, transform and
transfigure nature. What may be frightening more than
the scale of the endeavor are the many stigmas attached
to it. Those can all be framed in the implications of
"artificiality."

What is the artificial? The man-made. We may have
on one hand the abhorrent and uninspired suburbias and,

down to the microcosms, the ugly little vase on the window sill. Or we may have the quasi-unreal beauty of a terraced rice farm of the Orient and the warmth of a teapot beautifully crafted. Artifice is man's peculiarity. That is what makes it invaluable and so difficult to implement with reverence. Modern man, as no others before, heaps impressive amounts of artificial non-entities all over the earth; symbols and grievances of the life he seems to treasure and here and there timidly or forcefully the rare fruits of love with endless codas of eclectic copies. Where will we get the sensitivity, the broadness, the depth, the sufficient grace to make us adequate to the task we have given ourselves? Knowledge of the degree available now is insufficient asset.

It may even be that we should postpone our intervention on nature (agriculture aside) as we should postpone our quest into the "practical" uses of physico-biochemistry until our mind shall evolve some better moral lucidity. The fact is that by shovel or by dozer we have and we are transforming the earth. It is more often a disfiguring than a transfiguring. Less power-endowed societies did or do a far less damaging job (by default?) and achieve also many heart-filling transfigurations.

Deprived by our own doing of the organic patience the agricultural society used to put into the transformation of the earth, provided instead with the still questionable possessions of an exhilarating power, powers that make man prone to childishness, it is only through the esthetic transfiguration that we may hope to bridge the impasse of hastiness and avoid the scarrings of earth too deeply and too finally (in man's frame of reference).

Some of the perils facing the land sculptor, in addition to casualness and dogmatism are . . .

*Scatterization* The physical containment of man's action upon nature is fundamental. Suburbia shows us that whatever sprawls indifferently in any and all directions and does not carry the stern and beautiful mono-valence of a prairie, desert, sea, plowed earth, forest . . . is a curse on both man and nature. Let's act intensely, not extensively. Let the outcome of cosmic patience (indifference) surround the clustered fruits of man, heartening or disheartening as they may be. If the origin was the indifferentiate, then one must try to move away from it by the creation of the differentiate: the fullness of man within the fullness of nature.

*Fragmentation*  Our industry has presented us with the most tempting variety of possibilities, the ever-increasing needs that manufacturing produces and advertisement sells. The thousands upon thousands of pseudo-functions for each, scores of products to saturate the demand. This puts each man in the middle of his own disproportionate storehouse. The preoccupation of how and when to use, how to dispose of, is as great as the preoccupation of how to purchase. The ensuing mental and physical inquietude, the reaching everywhere-nowhere, is portrayed by the atomized environment of which the landscape made by man is one aspect.

*Complication*  Complication is the sister of fragmentation. The complicated should be left to the technological means. Guidance for modest abilities should be entrusted to integrity, coherence, respect for the simple, the "natural." The trust on some elementary rules. Generally, the sensitivity toward the land and water ecological balance will per se be the surest guidance toward harmonious solutions.

It would seem then that a dialectic exists between the need to conform to the laws nature is constructing and the inner laws that each creative man has to follow and conceive at the same time on his own. This has been so from the origins and the answer may reside in the necessity of going about life not by brute force, but by transfiguring fortitude.

# BACK TO NATURE?

I will be the first to advocate a return to nature, but my understanding of nature both in general and in detail is foreign to the used and abused slogans. When I think of natural man, my senses and my mind work out a world that I must label, if that were useful, as radical and conservative. Radical, because I must step back into the context of nature (not the appearance of it) so as to anchor myself to the roots of things. Conservative, because in my ignorance, a portion of the mountainous ignorance of the species, I take as my first duty to do the least I can of anything that might upset that balance I see and yet do not comprehend. Conservative and radical, because the little I see which is unequivocal in the evolution of life, I want to apply unequivocally to the furthering of it. The one thing I see also is that the way nature moves and the way we go are not congruent.

What if one seriously (even if ignorantly) looks at nature? Does it really say what we love to hear? What does nature (mineral and biological) say that is truly unequivocal and undeniable?

*The geophysical world is a changing but not an evolving world because of its ever-present perfection. Each of its stages is perfectly logical and formulable also. The faults appearing in it with the inception of life are the cracks from which evolution sprouts.*

1. It says that it is not a loose aggregation of happenings acting by sheer bulk, undisciplined and unpredictable, but that it is instead a formidable "machine," a machine rigorously self-regulating and fastidiously sensitive to change.

2. It says that nature's effortless grace is not spontaneous but is the end result, or in fashionable terms a spin-off, of its unrelenting grinding away at the inertial tide of entropy and amorphization. (Where refinement of nature is absent, regression is at work and with it, and, not just euphemistically, the vise of fate closes on the effusion we call "life.")

3. It says that nature is the birth and the brooding of endless gropings. It is the live-dead bed of myriads of consuming and consumed monads. It is, in its look, the outer membrane of an incredible creature, multiple and congruent, harsh and impassionate, dreadfully strict, rigorously unforgiving, unbelievably complex.

4. It says that nature's romantic flavor is in the eyes of the beholder. In fact, if the romantic spicing dislodges its substance, the romantic becomes the melancholy and the isolation booth of sentimentalism neatly separates intelligence from reality. The miracle of beautiful nature is indeed infinitely more massive than arcadia sings of it.

5. It says that nature is the effusion, deafening and life-hungry, of a fantastic diaspora in myriads of diverse fruits, a self-fulfilling process, an iron fist sprouting ineffable flowers.

6. It says that nature is our maker and our undoer. It surges within every one of us, flourishing in and spending us. It is our prime consumer.

7. It says that nature is massive, everlasting, ever-reaching. It is rational, just and logical.

To reinsert man then within such nature is something quite different from the domesticated and affluent tarzan-

*The evolutionary process is a process of interiorization of reality into the consciousness, albeit, the re-creation of itself. The spirit is this consciousness in action, the action being the making of ever more centered, imploded, complex, miniaturized wholes.*

ism we seem to wish. If "simple" nature needs a rigorous ecological discipline to work successfully, complex man needs an ultra-rigorous discipline to succeed. That this might be anathema and highly unfashionable does not faze nature. It does, however, quite directly despoil, degrade, destroy her fine ecologies (on earth) and, what should be of some interest for man, it predisposes the setting for man's extinction. Indeed, nature herself will simply, if not quietly, pinch the burning wick and kill the human flame to end the looting and the irrationality of man's action.

## COMPLEXITY

That an exponentially greater discipline for the human ecologies is needed is in the nature itself of man's genesis. As man moves into his infancy, the more complex the phenomenon man becomes. More and more he becomes individually the core of an enormously extensive and intensive process. He becomes social and cultural or, alternatively, a relic. But the more complex the single and the associated processes become, the more numerous and complex the interactions, that is to say, the necessary informations, distributions, connections, feedback, storing, etc. Thus, the more indispensable are timing and preparedness, swiftness and cogency, appropriateness and dimensioning, measure and frugality—efficiency in other words. Of all of those the biological man as an individual is gifted (*conditio sine qua non*). Of all of those the social animal, the collectivity, is pauper.

This social animal, a para-organism at least if not yet a fully constituted creature, is perhaps the only animal in the making for which nature has relinquished the planning if not the supervising. Indeed here man seems to be in charge as of that turn of events that has made his brain a dimension above animality. The planning has been trusted in his faltering hands. What, after eons of struggle, he has not yet truly grasped is that the same "savage" rigor of instrumentality is expected of his creation: society.

How dare we then, for instance, even whisper of the city as the fruit of a free-for-all, as a creature of change left to the randomness of individual idiosyncrasies? It is pure madness, the scale and massiveness of which makes for a perversion of global (terrestrial) nature.

A return to nature is just the opposite of what it is pictured to be. It is a radical insertion of the society of man in the biosphere according to the rules of the game. It is definitely not the desperate diaspora of the megalopolis and the suburbias. It is the rediscovery of the congruence between us and the structure that sustains us and is our maker. It is the alter ego of our species—nature: rational, just, rigorous. It is the careful and reverent planning of our inroad into a miracle of equanimity that has carried and developed itself for some billions of years.

## THE UNREAL

I am sorry to say that the flower children are out of all of this as much as the Madison Avenue slickers, the self-assured executive, the fabulous technocrats, the abstract general, and the political meddlers. None of them has an inkling of what is about them. None of them, as long as they carry on the masquerade, will get to dip a conscious finger into the torrential river of structure and blood that is sweeping them into oblivion.

If on the side of the establishment I see only callousness working out its own nemesis, on the side of the anti-establishment I see melancholy and nostalgia, the expectation of a garden of Eden that never had any truth to itself anyway.

On the other hand, radicalism is just what apocalypse is not. In fact, in the shortened perspective of history, pre-human billions of years included, the warping of the technological instrument that goes on under our eyes

might well end to be itself an apocalyptic moment, the
short flame of notoriety of the man-grinder. The "Hey,
here I am," half-sung, half-sobbed, followed by the un-
ending silence of a dumb universe.

## PAUPERISM AND GREED

For the radical world I think of, the obsolescence of
our hardware is just about complete and, as we identify
so much with it, so it seems that we ourselves too have
an irresistible bent on obsolescence. Collective greed might
be the *deus ex machina*. Collective greed can sustain itself
only by collective forgery. Collective forgery, fraudulence,
makes collective shabbiness. Collective shabbiness is a
chronic form of pauperism and the condition it expresses
is hard to amend. The corporated consumption economy
is the great solicitor of greed. "Your greed is my power"
the motto goes. Enthroning greed on the coffins of value,
the corporate power manipulates and consigns the boun-
ties of the earth to the dump grounds encircling the
settlements of greedy man (the nemesis).

What of our senses? Long awash in the fraudulent
pseudo-efficiency they crave, the flavor they taste is the
taste the robot rejoices in. We crave for what we are,
and what we are is the fruit of our craving. We do also
crave for a silly, nonexistent kind of nature. Maybe we
are silly, "nonexistent."

I feel it is my concern not to put up with those trends
but to go on with what I think is real and not a shadow
on the cavern wall. Environmentally speaking, the conception of social containers . . . the towns and cities that
are congruent to what society is meant for and can find
realization within the unavoidable rules of matter-energy.

As I suggested above, the proposition is radical and in
the long run it does away with both the megalopoly of
today and the suburbia of today and tomorrow. It does
away with them not for the sake of novelty, but because

both of them do not withstand the test of life, as they are structurally inimical to it. The topography of a man-made nature is the key to a working and developing society. What we have now is chaos and dereliction, two parameters totally inimical to living matter. Our troubles are not troubles of detail, they are core troubles. With the full advent of industrialization, we have embarked on a ship unable to withstand the assaults of the storm that surrounds it. In fact, we are navigating without a ship on homemade, extravagant rafts. The cunning and cleverness they might exhibit is of little avail. They do not amend the chronic unfitness that victimizes them.

Naturally, I do not say I have the answer because the answer would include the salvation of the present and next generations. This is not possible even in the most favorable of circumstances. What I think I have is a key to the right door. Beyond the door everything has to be done. But there I think we could find the guidelines for a renaissance of society. In a way, those guidelines are genetically imprinted on the key, inasmuch as the key is not a subjective finding or a game but one of the most pervasive rules observed by "nature." One way to put it is this, and with it I close: In any given system, the most complex quantum is also the liveliest. In any given system, the liveliest quantum is also the most miniaturized.

*The sun, that utterly savage chemistry, that instant hell, that monstrous furnace, that most unlikely generator of life . . . it is the focal, indispensable, essential origin, nurturer, developer of life, consciousness, reflection, spiritualization . . . evolution.*

# THE INNER AND THE OUTER IN ARID LAND

We can think of the arid land as dried up seas more than we can think of a sea as of an inundated desert. The cause of this preferential assessment, one condition being the deprivation of the other—aridity as deprivation of wetness—is quite probably in the make-up of life, which, as we all were surprised to find out in first grade, is preponderantly made of water. Aridity as deprivation of wetness but not vice versa is the first assessment of this paper.

Of all the substances we know, and more than any and all of them together water has the right to be called the primary media of life. We might consider this to be the second assessment since its very central implication is that fluidity, ubiquity, adaptability, pervasiveness, conductivity, motility are in and of life.

From life's position then, the seas and the desert are antithetical. In both of these, life, made of water and voids judiciously sprinkled with other substances, has to fight for its own identity and perpetuity. In the seas, the

*Water is not nourishment, it is the indispensable presence, the necessary media, the most pervasive building block. Of such nature must be other medias that go for the construction of a mental universe.*


*There is a large irrelevance in many of the "inoffensive" doings of man. One of these is the suburban limbo. There life is loosing to entropy, spirit is loosing to matter, light to obscurantism.*

battle (the aspect of it pertinent to this paper) is to keep out the saline fluid not perfectly matching the fluids of life's own composition (they are a "deviation" from the original broth and the naked proto-life suspended in it). In the desert, the battle is to keep in its own strictly measured and cunningly guarded fluids, an innovation whose occurrence was nothing less than the interiorization of the sea, achieved by every single organism, the actual fantastic invention of a wet, personalized universe for the advent of each individual organism.

## LIFE AS A WET UNIVERSE

As the planet has its own outer seas, not more than a fluid veil charged with chemicals, so the organism is an association of "spherical" seas, containing the fragments of solid matter disposed in structural, operative and interlocking marvels. The temperature, the composition and the morphology of each sea is rigorously maintained within strict limits. It would appear then evident that the enmity of life of the land environment, and more pertinently of the arid land environment, is far more acute than the enmity of the seas as the seas and the living belong to a wet universe; the arid land belongs to a water-deprived universe.

To reinforce this situation there is the fact that the sea is not only the environment for beings made of myriads of miniaturized seas, but it is also to a great degree the most pervasive logistical agent serving such beings. Not an irrelevant point as, when dealing with the urban life, logistics come out to be at the crux of the matter. Water is the carrier of the food and the wastes whose consumer and excretor are the animal and vegetal organisms. It is the most complete delivery system that ever existed on earth. It not only delivers to but also in the organism immersed in it. The sea might be not only the greater purveyor of life but also, and because of this special situation, its most dreadful incantator.

*If this is the last act we live in, then life is poorly justifiable. Its failures are too great and its inception swung too wildly and cruelly on creatures (and things?). If this (what we are in) is the origin of a quasi-infinite process, life has on its side both bottomless wells of suffering and radiant swells of joy. A third alternative is the grim technocratic embalming where the mechanics would run smoothly and reverence would be dead.*

So it is that the seas are the great caldron of the living and also why such living might be relatively uneventful. But while the seas are or might be responsible for relative dullness out of lack of greater challenges, the arid and the frozen lands are certainly responsible for emptiness and dread. One has only to spend the noon hours of a summer day in the desert, or a day on the frozen tundra, to grasp physically and conceptually the enormity of life's handicaps vis-à-vis the monstrously inimical nature and the added terrors of spatial infinity and temporal endlessness.

## PRECARIOUSNESS OF LIFE

What degree of folly sits then at the center of man's mind to envision himself settled in such an enemy territory? The folly is named "technology" and it is not sheer folly either, just one of the existential (fatal?) question marks besetting man.

With desert nomads or Eskimos the tenuous life they lead is rigorously governed by technological know-how: animal husbandry and domestication, and hunting techniques, to name three. It is to the everlasting glory of all men that in the prison of determinism in which they found themselves, they both could transfigure their survival, even if sparely and hardly more than hypothetically, into an esthetic experience.

Is our quasi-self-adjourning and exhilarating technology giving us a power and a prowess less hypothetical than theirs, or is it our exercise with it as ephemeral as a desert mirage?

Can we really bend the time-spacing ongoing of the desert and the tundras to our service or is our opulent and only apparently middle-class-shut-off-from-the-real-life very different (though infinitely bloodier) from the appearing-disappearing of the lichens and spores scattered and dormant in the stillness of a harsh mineral universe?

*The epitome of segregation is amorphism. The coming together of identical events (the lily-white congregation) whereby each monad encased in its own fears is identical to all others. No grouping becomes possible that does not have the simple character of a multiplicity of sameness. No organ or organism then but aggregation, i.e. repetitiousness, amorphism.*

*The automobile began as a toy and has remained so. It is mesmerizing the toy maker and the toy user, us. It is mesmerizing the inner and the outer. A toy to do business with has become the obstacle to the business of survival. The automobile is not a mixed blessing. It is an apocalyptic example of mindless logistics and technological savagery.*

And will our doing be as stubbornly persistent in its sway of torpor and suspended life? Is our desert life a durable and endurable thing? Quite possibly only under certain definite rules. Luckily, those same rules are also present whenever the social and cultural life of society appears. Indeed, they are more of a behavior to which the process of life is conditioned than a ruling and codified set of premises. The behavior that makes of any discrete phenomenon an ever-enlarging and beneficial one, when present, or a granular and destructive one if absent. This behavior is the constant increase of complexity of the living phenomenon (from the protozoans to man) and the corresponding contraction-miniaturization of the instrument needed by it. Very generally the situation is destructive where the phenomenon is of a segregative nature in as much as such condition rules out the complexity of the whole by cutting itself or part of itself out from the most comprehensive situation. In such case both the segregated and the situation are diminished. The ecological dilemma is, by the way, all there. Ultimately it is the energetic default in segregation, be it mental or physical, that is the built-in deficiency of atomism. "Wastefulness" is a fair name for this failing. That which does not belong to what surrounds it is lost to it. A great waste, but not the only one, because of the energy robbed from the whole by the single. Parenthetically in this light, the car is the great villain of the century, quite possibly the greatest villain of all times.

Granular performance (isolation) is counter-productive and cannot sustain itself without an exorbitant expense of energy, energy that must be borrowed from the extra-granular. It is then quite natural that depletion and exhaustion surround the granular performance, which, by the way, is descriptive of suburbia in general and of suburbia in arid lands in particular.

We are not tuned to the larger system that contains us. Nor is the ecological frenzy of the present, an ecological wafer from the temporal and spatial mass of ecology, of great significance. The ecological role is historical like anything else. In the light of history (evolution), its meanings and its lessons are quite different from the instant takes we make of it.

Snatching a slender fiber of personal history away from the gigantic flow of the biological is to hold the willful on a path of destiny. The lack in assertion of centered willfulness forgoes the individual. The lack of personal destiny forgoes man as an evolutionary phenomenon.

LOSS OF AIM

The suburban fragmentation is definitely part of the larger mirage of freedom and independence unhinged from the pervasive and stringent demands of that reality now fashionably called "ecosystem." The "negation" is indeed far more encompassing as it invests not only the instrumentality of which the ecosystem is one of the larger voices but also the aim itself of anthropogenesis. The emergence of the age of the ultra-rational, of the cultural, is negated by the homogenization of the two-dimensional aggregate of slumbering monads we call "suburbia."

The ecological viciousness of the suburban diaspora promotes itself into a death wish within the context of an extreme climate. It is not in our power nor in our right to submit parceled life to the dissipating violence of the arid, the hot, the cold. If and when we so do, we put ourselves out of the congruence among the living and between the living and the mineral. The end result is, sooner or later, disaster—the double disaster of brittleness and absurdity.

In the arid land, man must go the way of the cacti: density, corposity, tri-dimensionality . . . all absent in suburbia. As I was trying to point out in the beginning, seas and deserts are two extremes. In the seas, life must fight to keep water inside its organism. In the arrested life of the desert where the green life rises from death for a short spell after every good rain and where animal life is in a deadly game of hide and seek between itself and the sun, the only (visible) living thing that goes on undaunted and defiant is the cactus. The cactus has a tough and quasi-impermeable skin and a body full of water, a body which is voluminous, solid, thick. In it the quotient surface volume is the smallest achievable in the vegetal kingdom. We would be mistaken if we compared the cactus to one organism, man, and say that those same characteristics are of man and that consequently

*The return to nature is about the opposite of what it is pictured to be. It is the rediscovery of congruence between the part and the whole. It is the reconnection of the speck to the enormity of the cosmos. But it is fundamentally the careful and reverent planning of one's own species into futures of ever higher degrees of improbability.*

*To construct is for man to affirm differentiation and to resist dissociation. The indifference of the universe "sponges" man even when he constructs. In fact, when he constructs purposelessly or maliciously, he simply masquerades emptiness with wastefulness. He works so as to perpetuate the indifference of the mineral cosmos, undermining at the core the dedication of life to "forming."*

man is made for the desert. The reasons are obvious. The dynamics and the intensity of the human organisms are incomparably more demanding than those of the cactus. Hence, the support systems for one are not comparable in scale and ecological impact to those of the other. The fact is that the social-cultural boundaries of man are where the "city limits are." Then the analogy is fruitful when the cactus is compared not to the single organism but to the body of society, that physical instrument we call the town and the city. They are, comparatively speaking, a most primitive organism, given yet to torpid life only dimly conscious of themselves; a fitting description of the cactus. (How often do we, part of the city, think as citizens?)

Villages, towns, cities of the arid land when and where they can be accepted by the ecological system must present themselves as large, tri-dimensional, self-sheltering bodies, interiorized seas of "wetness," shade and logistics, not flat oases hammered by the hot air into the hotter dust of the earth or nailed frozen into its frozen crust. In both cases, the price is not worth the chance and the lingering life that they might sustain has no future.

*The occurrence of the mental "explosion," that is to say, the powerful thrust of the mental processes beyond the physical barriers of the mineral world, is directly dependent on the contraction of the physical tools adopted by the mind. It is as if the spirit of which matter is tenuously pervaded would come "to life" and activate a reality only when extruded out of the structure of matter itself by the formidable pressure of complexification—miniaturization.*

As an illustration, perhaps it is of some use to go to the limit and consider an urban system forced to exist in the harshest of all environments, the non-environment of space, a city asteroid, an asteromo. Here are some of the eminent characteristics of such a hypothetical city:

1. Rigorous confinement within a membrane separating being from non-being.

2. The inward orientation of a community physically standing head to head along the axis of rotation.

3. The coincidence of emptiness with death, the loneliness of the living lost in the solid black of the universal mega-machine.

4. The constant pace of the transformations in the details of the system within a given and generally unchanging macro-system (the asteroid).

5. The transformism of instrumentality to accommodate different functions.

6. The definition of its own ecology and the balance of the general performance in it.

7. The self-reliance necessary for a system almost abandoned to its own resources in a hostile environment (the absence of one).

8. The roundness of the tasks to perform energetically, biologically, mentally.

9. The evident dependence of everyone on everyone else, making the whole unmistakably an organism whose organs perform given but "fluid" tasks.

10. The coincidence of equity and congruence in a microcosmos where to be a free agent coincides with complete responsibility.

11. Finally, the rigor of the rules of complexity-miniaturization reflected by all of those characteristics.

## THE PERSONAL, THE EVOLUTIONARY

All this dramatizes the stark fact that we are as relevant with our lives as much and no more than how we make

Man of "himself" is prometheus-bound. The bondages being the social, political, cultural, personal, entanglements within the species. Man of the universe is prometheus-bound to the power of two for whom the human bondages are overcast or underlines by the lithosphere, the biosphere, and are immersed in the immense vats of the cosmos. Man of the universe is the only man who has a future.

The ecology "subspecies evil man" will simply be a more "mineral" ecology, and remain so until the self-extinction of the family of man. Then in her own quiet, formidable and unarrestable way, nature will swing back to the prehuman condition, a little wiser? A little shorter in future, with the episode of man archived among the other countless ones, one of the shortest, and most daring.

Randomness can be defined as the freedom of the non-purposeful. If one denies purpose in man, one is right in saying that he behaves at random. Then our freedom is license.

sense not only within the context of the us and now, with their loads of fairness, justice, well-being, etc., but also within the larger context of an ever-present supporting or crushing nature, the universe of matter, energy and life that has made us single-handedly so to speak, in our tortured and fantastic beginning and which is no less portentously overriding any folly we perpetrate, in spite of our ignorance of it. We must remember that the time beat of reality as a whole is incommensurably longer than our single little flickers, but that at the same time is the cumulative effect of what those flickers are and do that puts the responsibility of the future, which is most of what life does with ourselves, square on the shoulders of each generation.

The enormity of our responsibility will reveal itself in the effects we will have caused many generations ahead of us. Our indifference means not only to be dimly alive but it means also to be killers in the most vicious of ways as it contains an ultimate negation of a future for the phenomenon of man.

A decision in terms of economic speculation of if and how to colonize arid lands is thus headed for nowhere to the same degree of any other decision to act disregarding the continuity of the real. This comes hard to practical man and it focuses exactly on the difference between the practical and the real.

## PRACTICAL MAN

What is practical for a corporation looking for cheap land to put up shop on, and low taxes to operate by, has no relation whatsoever to the reality of an ecological tightrope walk between being and not being. The expediency of the former we call wrongly the realism of practical man. It is indeed the shortsightedness of a confused and an arrogant species equating short-term feasibility with desirability. We do our things very much

*If the indifference of the physical is registered in the laws of great numbers, the biological is fundamentally the injection of the element of improbability within the ordained probable.*

*To keep the miracle of life going on in self-creating, the rational base of life is faced with awesome logistical problems.*

*Man has in his power of reflection the instrument of a self-creating "God." Such an infant God, distant offspring of the trigger god of fate is the super-structuralizer of a structured universe.*

on a hit-and-run tactic while our strategies are bankrupt. The hit-and-run tactic of the developer is a modern equivalent of piracy and what he leaves behind is a social misery, cultural death and ecological disaster, and that is a fair description of many deeds of practical man.

## REAL MAN

Inner and outer in arid lands must be eminently co-ordinated or the conflict that results will never bring victory to the more discrete of the two, man. Evolutionary coherence indicates the road to take: the road of high co-ordination, great density, high performance, minimal waste, limited pollution, respect of land and its subtle balances . . . all of these basic elements for an urban, social, cultural and compassionate life. That seems to convey a paradox: there where life is the least "natural" is where life will succeed only when most fully and most intensely sought and pursued. The same paradoxical stigma (of improbability) labeling any creative act. The greater the challenge, the most courageous and passionate the response.

I do not aim to give numbers or percentages, though in the final analysis, I believe those will be impressive. I do want to present a position which I believe to be the only one to withstand the crushing weight under which man, the highest and most responsible form of life, is operating.

For quite too long we have played with expediency as if it were a virtue. As we are harvesting exactly what we obtusely sowed for generations, we see now the enormity of our assumptions and presumptions. We will put order to our house or we will have no house to work with. The challenge of the arid land is strong and unforgiving. We will make something out of it within the congruence which ingrains the living with the non-living or else.

The fantastic assumption that economic speculation or

freakish technology is codifying and sanctifying our operations has produced obscurantism and depersonalization, which is why the ecological alarm bells are ringing. If our paradigms are not truly compassionate, universally so, we are marked for the slaughterhouse. Nor will the universe have the smallest jolt out of that, but life will; an irreparable jolt, as life has no reverse gears. It is an anthropogenesis pointing upward, beyond itself.

# THE QUIET GREED

Man today is hard-pressed by the following conditions:
   The population tide
   The ecological debacle
   The waste syndrome
   The pollution problems
   The disposal problems
   The energy-depletion problems
And there is overriding and fulfilling, the behavior of evolving life rigorously trained in every one of its manifestations by increasing complexity and, consequent to it, a contraction of its instrumentality. These are all converging factors toward a reordering of priorities and toward a refocusing of our intervention in the balance of that thin and delicate system we call the biosphere. The Arcological Commitment I am proposing is at the focal point of this convergence. That is to say, the scope of my proposals has to be taken in the context of the human, urban and ecological crisis. Fifteen years ago all the elements making up this crisis were present, working and evident, but the gov-

*If by dole and bribery affluence can instigate the continuity of flow, the flow is that portion of things and doings not yet prey to opulence's freeze. Opulence is a pollutant that pollutes itself on the double level of matter and mind. It fouls the environment and it fogs the mind.*

ernment, the industry, the universities and the public were indifferent to them. In a very real sense, things are no better today. We seem constantly and hopelessly late in recognizing and responding to the challenges we pose to ourselves. The crux of the matter, intentionally or not, is kept under cover.

1. Expediency is still the password.
2. The health of the family of man is not an end in itself.

For the necessary limits of this chapter, the two can be joined together by saying that the pollution of the environment will not recede if not accompanied by a recession of the pollution of the soul. It is an overdue crisis of conscience; a massive and collective crisis of conscience, individually carried and individually powered.

## MENTAL POLLUTION

The empty beer can, the discarded napkins, the burned fuel, the ever-growing size and number of the garbage can, the asphalt and cement plague, the paradox of the car, the draining of energy into irrelevance, the voraciousness of our comfort are the fruits that materialism piles up around the ever-weakening stalk of our conscience and our sensitivity. The dirty skies are dividends of poor judgment, the filthy rivers are the drains for the dirty linens of a callous human family, the devastated landscape is the wasteland of a life unfit for living. Man's genius is decaying within the process of ecological decay.

As the soul of things so hastily denied by administrators, bureaucrats and technicians drains away in us and around us, the soul of man, withering but still alive, is the only real and only hope. But this soul is in desperate search for a structure, for a shelter, for a home, in fact for a topography . . . (the city) . . . and for a scope.

The true pragmatist must disengage himself from practical man as practical man is demonstrating over and over again his unfitness as a leader and decision maker. His

*We stare at the face of the Big Hypocrisy and slowly but surely surround ourselves with the paraphernalia of death. Affluence and opulence are not viable statuses. They are not, not because they might not be able to bring about equity (indeed they could for a brief spell), but because they are incapable of congruity within the life of the biosphere. The wealth of the mind does not imply that such kind of affluence can be transferred to the material universe for the production of an opulent status of affairs. Life and opulence are not compatible inasmuch as life is a quest while opulence is a status. The state of opulence is halted life.*

legs are far too short for the stern stride of reality. Government, administration, Pentagon, Detroit, Wall Street, Madison Avenue, mass marketing, mass selling are all enclaves for practical man . . . We are all practical man, and by trimming back to cash and mortgage, respectability and comfort all of our best impulses we are left with the cinders and the ironies reserved to all bystanders.

There is a quiet greed holding us to a quasi-fanatical dedication: The degradation of the earth that sustains us. Our greatest problem is to face this and find for it a resolution or prepare ourselves for the ultimate graveyard.

## AFFLUENCE

The official and proud name of our quiet greed is affluence. It is not paradoxical anymore to say that affluence is not causing pollution, but it *is* pollution. Whenever we try to analyze affluence, we find its faults minor, its flaws accidental and its shadows negligible. The analysis is usually done by one of two kinds . . . the affluent or the affluent-to-be. One is in the midst of it (often born in it), and cannot see it for real. The other will be in it, with luck, and does not know it yet. Only post-affluent man knows it and can read it.

To become post-affluent, we must radicalize our thinking. And the radical man seeks the geology on which to root the structure of his universe. He must, not just metaphorically, become ecologically conscious and earthly relevant. Then he will start to see affluence for what it is: opulence. Opulence is a condition, not a process. It is a plateau of which life becomes the floor and on which any better thing is smothered. We know now that affluence-opulence for all (soon four billion of us) would be death for all, as the biosphere could not accept a debacle of such proportion. Now that we, the United States, 6 per cent of the population of the planet, consume and destroy 50 per cent of its exploited resources, we stare darkly from

the hole of parasitism. Parasitism has grown at the expense
of the soul and has fed beautifully on greed, bigotry and
ignorance. Parasitism is literally devouring our future.

## ENERGY

Our quiet greed is eminently a lonely fact. As one seems
incapable of activating ideas and producing the running
sap of culture, one sinks into the habit of collecting hardware and the access to the physical energy they demand.
One slowly barricades oneself from the unknown and the
alien by one's own heap of possessions and prowess. This
is a lonely world surrounded by a diaspora of identical
and identically lonely worlds. The loneliness intrinsic to
the condition of man, a speck of consciousness lost within
the deterministic mega-machine of the universe does not
need this kind of redundance, if we keep also in mind
that in the end this same greed becomes pervasive, brutal
and savage in the enormities of war, defense budgeting
and their technological sorcery.

Ecologically this means that while colossal amounts of
matter and energy are depleted, and energy is not self-
reproducing but only transferable while degrading, the
energy of the mind is really left idle. But it is just this kind
of energy that, if idle, degrades. The mental energy,
knowledge, is self-creating when given to others: the
teacher is the inexhaustible source of energy that grows
in itself by pouring itself into the mind of the pupils.

Materialism is the lopsided equation where the limited
physical energy available to man is burned away sense-
lessly and the mental energy, explosively powerful, is kept
in the dungeons of a callous life. One should remember
on the path cut by knowledge is growth. On the path cut
by physical energy are ashes (pollution). The ecological
dilemma is to be framed there, if it is to be understood and
cared for.

FRUGALITY

The future of life is in the hand of frugal man. The frugal man is only occasionally in agreement with the man who can produce more with less (industrial efficiency) because so much of what he produces is irrelevant, i.e., ecologically and humanly negative.

The frugal mind is eminently ethical, while producing more with less is eminently practical. Only when the practical finds common ground with the ethical have we congruence and the meeting with reality within it. The crucial problem is not to invent and produce a less pollutant car, to filter all the smoke stacks, to dispose better of our wastes, etc. The crucial problem is to bring the individual mind to the choice of a structural congruence within nature, a congruence whose first demand is for leanness and substance, not opulence and fraud.

But to despair of man because of his defaults is also fraudulent, because it looks at the present in the wrong context. We do not stand at the end of an abortive process that will be concluded and forgotten. We are part of a miraculous chain of events that started more than four billion years ago and has seen the most incredible things happening (in the last few moments of its development: the advent of man). We can justly say that the whole history of man is in the future. But this will not come to be automatically or randomly. The future will be the willful and structural construction of itself in the actual process of self-creation. It will definitely not come along as a by-product of an opulent society and the quiet greed breeding it and bleeding it white.

It is quite possible that the future of man will be or will not be, depending on the ability or not of all of us to comprehend not only how general and pervasive is the predicament of man and how courageous and radical the response to the challenge must be, but also how incredibly rewarding the future of life can be and ought to be if the challenge is seen as the catalyst for fulfillment.

# POLLUTION AS ENTROPY
## (Gigantism as Pollution)

One abused word to be found in this chapter is pollution. That it might be a fashionable word because shallow, or that it is shallow because it is fashionable, is a matter of conjecture. I am using it to present the dilemma of life versus non-life. That the fashion in which life conquers non-life might not be a fashionable subject is as good as any indication of the crack fissuring planetary reality down the middle.

I am identifying pollution[1] in its comprehensiveness to entropy,[2] and asentropy as the opposite of entropy. As there are two extremes from which to consider the in-

[1] *pollution* . . . emission of semen at other times than in coition, defilement, desecration, profanation, corruption. (Webster's Third New International Dictionary)

[2] *entropy* . . . the ultimate state reached in the degradation of the matter and energy of the universe: state of inert uniformity of component elements: absence of form, pattern, hierarchy, or differentiation. (Webster's Third New International Dictionary)

divisible universe, the extreme of "inanimate matter" and the extreme of "animate matter," the physical and the metaphysical, I try to be even-handed and look with the "eyes" of both. What I find is that what is pollution is also asentropy for one extreme, the extreme of inanimate matter, and what is pollution is also entropy for the other extreme, the extreme of animate matter.

Then entropic pollution is the process which works toward conditions of accelerated entropy, death. The asentropic "pollution" is that process, the becoming, which works toward conditions of decelerated or reversed entropy, life. The asentropic "pollution" is such from the point of view of a hypothetical mineral god who sees his plans for a totally amorphous universe sabotaged by life, the spirit. The pious "environmentalist" works most of the time hopelessly at semblances of asentropy, lost within the entropic pollution cloud, as a man pretending that he is going home because on the ship going north he is walking south, the direction to his home. The compassionate "environmentalist" works tirelessly at turning the ship around, only secondarily concerned for who or what on the ship goes where, as consciously or not, willfully or not, all and everything moves south where the ship is going, "home." The ship stands not for the down-trodden cosmos but for that fraction of it, the biosphere, for instance, falling under his responsibility.

For us, life-spirit, the two theses are thus: entropic pollution, the unwinding of life, or asentropic life, the genesis of trans-matter, not in the sense of twentieth-century progress but in the sense of 3 billion years of evolutionary etherealization. Given this frame of reference, and no matter how dogmatic the stance might appear, there is really no alternative between the two. This is, by the way, why pietism and compassion do not coincide. Until we are able to see the lighthouse of the home port, the results of our effort remain utterly precarious and the goal recedes ever more into the "probable" (the statistical). Nor must we be mystified by the analogy. There is not such a thing as the lighthouse or home. What there is is far more glorious and uncomfortable. It is an ever sharper tooling of life vis-à-vis itself and cosmos and, springing out of such tooling, the creation, slow and pain-filled as much as joy-filled, of the universe of the spirit, the asentropic universe, the true anti-pollutant reality.

Therefore, the only honest, realistic, pragmatic question is: Does this or that doing foster the spirit or does it not? If it does not, it is "authentically" certain that it is a pollutant. If it were not so, the whole, the totality of the phenomenon of life from the purely "mineral" ecology of the original solar system to the ecology of today, 15 January 1972, is a fiction, a farce, a fraud, a devastation, not extant, non-real. Then each of our actions, especially those actions collectively performed, must be seen through a different "truth filter" as if looking at a landscape through infrared light. Instances:

Item 1)   Does the butchering (and what precedes and follows it) of a whole generation of domestic animals, fowl, hogs, sheep, cattle, etc., 365 days per year, year in and year out, foster the spirit? Very probably, yes, if by such tamed savagery homo sapiens is able to heighten the intensity of life and consciousness. There is, there, yet a debt of man toward life which we should feel in the marrow of our bones. This marrow itself is a gift from superb specimens of asentropic pollution, the slaughtered animals. It is only if the marrow of our bones is sustaining a greater and more compassionate intensity than that of the slaughtered animal that we atone our debt as by being what we are we "become" the entelechy of the butchered animal. And, by the way, isn't the outcry over the fate of the coyote and the eagle, rightly or wrongly accused of disrupting the asentropic battle slightly hypocritical, and is our indignation commensurate with the massiveness of our slaughtering?

Item 2)   Given the landscape of Europe, let's say 20,000

years ago, blanketed by forests, and the Europe of today almost uninterruptedly farmed, would we find more ethe-realization among the saber-tooth tiger, mammoth, bison, bears and trees than today, even the todays of 1914 or 1939? If we say yes, we must carefully disconnect ourselves from everything which is of "civilized" nature, that is to say, all that which is human and return to the innocence of the animal. Step forward, please, if any one of us is so inclined. I, for one, will stone you, betraying the spirit, you, a true "entropic pollutant."

Item 3) Is the affluent-opulent dynamism of runaway technology entropic pollution or asentropic "pollution," more amorphism or more spirit? As affluent-opulent, yes, an entropic pollutant; the discomfort of creation does not thrive on chemical, ecological, physiological and intellectual Bufferin. When, for instance, we drive a car, we do not simply pollute the air because of the inefficient power plant we use, we pollute in proportion to every pound of material that has been produced and processed to make the car and to make it run . . . from crank case to glove compartment, from roadways to bridges, from parking lots to gas stations, from assembly line to car graveyard. We then better have a good reason not only for turning the engine on but for producing and buying a car, or for that matter anything else. As an instrument frugally implemented and freeing the mind by caring for the body, technology is non-pollutant, it is asentropic.

There is then, such a thing as a ship of fools, exchanging insults and ephemera, pious and lacrimal, or waspish and despotic, oblivious of their calling, or their debt, of the indispensable atonement for that which is parasitic in the make-up of man (Item 1), oblivious of the majestic and awesome thrust of the whole of life, expectant from the human mind ever greater miracles of consciousness, understanding, creation. How dare we, so pious, philistines, cynics, beat our breasts and warp the future in one and the same?

If what we see tells us unequivocally, beyond any existential ambiguity, that in this earthly cosmos the displaying of time and history has caused some of the mineral stuff, which in gaseous and consequently liquid and solid state had been the only component of a reality, dumb, insensible, corpuscular, blind, unconscious, entropic, that is to say proto-alive, if it has caused some of this stuff to metamorphose into consciousness, then there is where we see that a vectoriality is establishing itself unequivocally and unambiguously. It is the asentropy for which entropy and pollution are one and the same.

To say that this vector, at this contingency of history, is smashing itself against the wall of a fatal nemesis, the contention of many pious environmentalists, is at least peculiar and certainly irrational. What is it that makes the present, today, the arbiter and the executioner of the immense tide of this earthly reality? Rejecting this, as we must, it then becomes necessary, the necessity of congruence and continuity, of self-preservation and development, of "satisfaction" and fulfillment, of revolution and evolution, that what is in the future has a methodological continuity with what is in the past, as it is the past which is the *only* extant methodology. The methodology the past has had constant recourse to in its evolution is: that which is simple develops itself into that which is complex and in so doing transcends itself into a new and more forceful context. Inasmuch as such "more" has to be sustained by a close, finite, energetic universe, it is ultimately mandatory that it must define itself by a better utilization of such universe. Only in this way is complexity a limitless undertaking, as it has the ability to become indefinitely more so by demanding ever smaller quanta of mass-energy to be itself. Such power of exponential metamorphosis is intrinsic to miniaturization. It is to be noted that this points to the at least theoretical possibility of a God point, containing in its "non-dimension" the totality of reality, an utterly complex, utterly miniaturized reality: pure spirit.

When such development comes to rest, the transcendence does not occur, the "vector" disintegrates, randomness takes over, minerality returns . . . entropy . . . pollution . . . death.

The progression is such a lengthy one and so crammed with miraclelike events that to dismiss it as a construction of the imagination is stupid or philistine. The tidal wall of the spirit has shaken the cosmos off its complacent, deterministic bearings, and the intellectual hypocrite cannot do a thing about it. He is utterly impotent vis-à-vis the vitalization of the earth. He himself in all his corrosiveness is a constituent monad of it.

On such premises, I would like to make the following propositions:

*Proposition No. 1* On the co-ordinate representing reality and without the need to know what reality is: at one extreme, the "entropic end," such reality might be defined, elementary, electro-magneto-gravitational, unconscious, unsensitive, amorphous, amoral. At the other extreme, the "asentropic end," such reality might be defined complex, psychosomatic, sensitive, differentiated, conscious, moral, spiritual.

*Proposition No. 2* It is inconceivable that the thrust of the asentropic extreme can be self-annihilation, as this is tantamount to saying that the purpose of life is to die. Of all the suppositions which life (the mind of man) can make about itself, the most senseless is that one is something in order to be the negation of such something. The biologist tells us that the whole of life can be seen as an endless struggle to find a more secure, less precarious way for life itself to "remain alive."

*Proposition No. 3* Of all manifestations of life we know of, the human species embodies more intensely than all others this thrust toward "ethereal life." Man has even invented immortality and invested it in supreme beings. Homo sapiens is more alive than the others, plants or animals, because:

1. He is conscious of himself and of his own action.
2. He has developed as non-specialized, as conceptualizer, as maker. He is the learning animal par excellence and, by far the most crucial aspect, he is "compassionate." He is the arrowhead of the vector, matter-spirit, in the direction of the spirit.

*Proposition No. 4* From propositions, 1, 2 and 3, it appears that the "gaseous state" (amorphous) of the early "formed" cosmos stands at the entropic end of the cosmic cycle. The spirit incorporated in man stands as the asentropic arrowhead of the spiral of life. One can then state that from the "point of view" of the mass-energy cosmos, asentropy is pollution, an annoying and embarrassing by-product of the cosmic megamachine. There is not such a point of view, as by the preceding proposition such cosmos is mindless. From the point of view of the spirit, whatever unwinds the spiritual spring of life is pollution. We are thus faced with two kinds of pollution: asentropic pollution, embarrassing to "pure matter," and entropic pollution, ever ready to overwhelm and annihilate life. Those two and only those two are comprehensive of the whole of reality we are so unwillingly steering at.

*Proposition No. 5* Both terms "asentropic pollution" and "entropic pollution" are redundant. On the co-ordinate presented in Proposition No. 1, the entropic end sees as pollution the interference of the asentropic end. Entropy pollutes life; asentropy "pollutes" non-life.

*Proposition No. 6* Then the horizontal, Brownian, objective view on the biosphere's condition must be discarded for the vertical (vectorial) evolutionary view (not Brahma but the Christ) and a lot of homework expects both the pious ecologist and the ruthless technologist.

*Proposition No. 7* In the vertical-vectorial view, the reverence for life does not, ever, imply the conservation of a "present" condition nor the restoration of a past condition, but the transcendence of the future working on the past and the present. Transcendence, the transformation of "more" matter into spirit, not forgetting that spirit is qualitative, not quantitative, which is, by the way, where the Catholic Church might be challenged. (Go and multiply . . .)

*Proposition No. 8*   There is a methodology to the "transformation" of matter into spirit. What is evident of this methodology is the direct dependence of the phenomenon on the complexity it can instrumentalize itself with. And there is an overwhelming documentation (evolution) of the fact that ultimately spirit is qualitative, thanks to the miraculous power of miniaturization humbly working at the nuts and bolts of complexity. This is the natural order of things, as life is totally dependent on information and the appropriate responses the information elicits about itself and itself as part of the environment.

*Proposition No. 9*   Speed, the swiftness by which information, building material and energy are transferred piggyback or without intermediary, is the key to process and growth. Speed, the swiftness by which the response in terms of matter (building blocks) and/or energy (the fuel) is dispatched where needed, is the key to survival and growth. Speed loads mass with energy. The greater the mass, the more brutal the "missile." The neutrino perforates the body at light speed without damaging it. A car at ten miles per hour destroys it. Speed that builds is the swift way to wholeness. Speed that kills is the swift way to granularity (entropy, pollution). Swiftness is really what is demanded by asentropy, not speed. It is the *sine qua non* of life. If swiftness cannot be achieved by speed, which is the case for any living thing, it can only be achieved by the alteration of the remaining parameter available; distance. Distance has to shrink so that swiftness prevails. Therefore, the mandatory need for miniaturization whenever a living phenomenon is in cause.

*Proposition No. 10*   Gigantism, not size but size relative to complexity, is entropic, pollution of the spirit. As the macro and the micro are constructed with the same modular bricks and those bricks commute and interact at limited speeds (speed of light as the known limit), the more they can do so the more they can make use of their affinities and versatility. We then see that macro molecules of the living tissue constitute a mini universe enormously packed with eventfulness, to which side the microscopic "mineral" molecule is a wasteland of dread and naught. Therefore, the larger of the two, thousands or more times over, is the more miniaturized of the two.

*Proposition No. 11* Sentiment fails man if at this point one rebels against the notion of miniaturization as the only path to spiritualization. One has to be blind to facts not to recognize that we, as all living creatures, are specifically, rigorously, unavoidably, beautifully, miraculously, concretely miniaturized universes. Take this characteristic out of life and what we have left is a dream, a fiction, a something well-illustrated by Walt Disney's dolls: simulation by oversimplification, deminiaturization. (Proposition No. 9)

*Proposition No. 12* Miniaturization, the instrument of complexity-spirit (the asentropy of the world), does not stop at the single organism, as "the group" has an identical if not greater need of integrating swiftness. The emergence of the spirit is only in a quasi-prenatal stage of development. It would be utter arrogance to maintain that we, homo sapiens 1972, are the flower, or worse the fruit, of such emergence. We are, at most, the first groping dendrils wedging themselves in the dark granularity of spirit's underpinnings. The future is literally the whole of life's evolution in time, space, power, but mainly in intensity. How else can we, life, create God? (I am literal, not euphemistic.)

*Proposition No. 13* There is a "collective" instrumentality, the correspondent structure in non-biological form of the soma in the animal kingdom. It is, in its more comprehen-

sive form, the city. The city of man, that is. To confuse the
city of man with the beehive or the anthill is folly. The city
is of civilization. There is no city where there is no man.
Therefore, the city is essentially and uniquely human. It is
asentropic (Proposition No. 3) to an enormously greater
power than the beehive, the anthill, the coral reef, etc.,
but it is, as they all are, an ultra-organism or transorgan-
ism . . . outdistancing as a whole the destiny, the fate,
the substance of the component individuals: bee, ant,
polypus, man. Crush the whole and the individual is lost.
*Proposition No. 14* Associative, co-operative, integrative,
implosive are the asentropic ways, the anti-pollution
modes. They are purposeful, personalizing, normative,
ontological-eschatological and they are necessarily "efficient." They do the most with the least. One mammal is a
synopsis of a whole coral reef. The consciousness which
can be added up as a sum total of the amount contained
in a coral reef is less than the amount detected in a small
mouse.
*Proposition No. 15* The individual effort of "imploding"
around the seed a co-operative organism is more than
analogically repeated in a "cosmic" scale where the total
semen of life, while genetically evolving, is painfully but
powerfully gathering, implosively, the universe of mass-
energy into one creature, temporarily earthly, futurely
transworldly. In between those two poles—the person,
present and realized, and the totality of the spirit, potential and improbable—stands the city of the present, a raw
prototype of what can be the Civitate Dei in its becoming.

# THE FLIGHT FROM FLATNESS
## (Thoughts for Elevator
## Manufacturers)

We, you and I, are interested in the same thing, though with different aims. My aim is a better access to a freer life by offering man an urban topography that has shed off a good deal of the dead weight of inefficiency. To achieve this is not possible if we persist in staying leashed to the center of the earth. Gravity sees to it that a leash is always going to be there, but it is up to us to make it more and more elastic. (It sprang to the limit and broke with the Apollo flights.) We will produce better urban environments only when we turn to the spaces above . . . layers upon layers (each about ten feet above the next), spaces for us to plan, organize, urbanize, humanize. Your aim could be to define the best hardware connecting those spaces for the transportation of peoples and things and for their interaction. It is my conviction that the more you know of the reasons why the thickening of our urban texture is the way to a better urban life the better you might be able to invent and perfect such hardware.

If history is a progression of improvements, and in the

long, long run this can hardly be denied, then it might well be written in the future that the place and the power now occupied by Detroit and the automobile might be substantially passed to those industries that most fore-sightedly have geared themselves for the flight from flat-ness. There ought to reside your aspirations and expec-tations, and there also might be your undoing as your brother's keeper if in your success you will forget the aim, man, and mysticize the instrument you are supposedly constructing for him. There is where the automobile in-dustry is now, and it will not take many years for history to condemn it as one of the scourges of the earth.

You might or might not want to see it this way, but the battle will be raging between the "horizontalist" and his triumphant horde of magic machines and the "verticalist" and his, at present, slim battalions of self-effacing (collec-tive) riding boxes and ramps. Perhaps you might also want to see if the title of rapid transit might not be your prerogative, inasmuch as rapid transit among the urban texture can mean only short time-space gaps and not the illusory pursuit of high speeds. Velocity is contradictory within the urban diaspora. It presupposes science fictions like instant acceleration and instant deceleration. It pre-supposes the submission of people, including children, ill people, the aged, etc., to many G's of pressure. It pre-supposes incredibly sophisticated and grimly expensive hardware . . . it presupposes utopia in its most fraudulent schemes.

There is where you are in agreement with the logistics of life, not against them as the horizontal performance is. This is not a paradox. Precisely because we individuals act horizontally, the spaces we need are like pancakes of many hundreds of square feet in area and only 8 to 10 feet thick. It follows that the worst way to connect effi-ciently such pancakes is to scatter them on one surface (suburbia is the classic example). The direct, efficient way is to stack them one on another. Your work is about the connecting fibers of such stacks. Connecting fibers not relying so much on speed but on the swiftness afforded by good engineering and the fundamental fact that your distances are measured in feet and always within the half mile at most and not in hundreds of feet and scores of miles which is the case of the horizontal traffic.

Traffic, by the way, in Italian means also a mess, and I would leave that term for the road. We will not kill the logistical inertia and the paralysis overcoming traffic at its peaks and everywhere in between by killing space through the mirage of velocity, but by killing distance, period. Hence, the excellence of the elevator transportation and the obsolescence of the road traffic.

The other asset of the vertical mode is that by being perpendicular to the performing flow, the activities within the pancakes, it serves them by perforating them. That is to say, it does its logistical tasks with the least amount of intrusion. It performs the talk frugally, in sharp contrast with the opulent and bloated mode of the automobile that results in a paralysis not limited to its task but extended to the whole body social.

As the future seems to be with you, you should try earnestly to be for the future. This extends your responsibility from the purely instrumental to the aims the instrument must foster. The arrogance of the automobile is the arrogance of the minds that power its productive and consumptive mechanisms. The self-effacing characteristic of the elevator will not dispense your industry from the attention it must pay to the congruence between the task and the total cost of its performance. The more self-effacing the instrument is, the more it comes close to the ideal performance. Miniaturization is one of the roads to unobtrusiveness as it is the road to the goal of putting more into less. The most fantastic example of this is naturally any biological organism in which analogy the city one day will be conceived. In it the vertical, slanted, radial and annular flow are the business of your business. So much so that you might want to invest some of your economic power to accelerate its advent.

"The flight from flatness" should be more than a good slogan. It stands for the unchaining of man from the topography of the earth at a moment when the earth itself is becoming too small for comfort. The dependence on the biosphere and the respect we owe to it demands a total reorganization of our communities from the village to the megalopoly, a reorganization along vertical vectors, the vectors you make hardware for. But as I don't like to see the task of man as a pure pursuit of comfort and health but as something far more exacting and exalting, I would close by saying that man is in need of the best instruments technology can give him so as to set the stage for his liberation.

# GOING TO NOWHERE, ANYONE?
## (The Airport, a Non-Place)

It is presumed by many that rapid transportation is an asset for mankind. I would submit from the beginning that in the physical diaspora of our urbanizing environment, rapid transportation, velocity, is not the means that will give the individual that reaching ability he ought rightly to expect. The solution of the general logistics of society will not be found in the co-ordinate of speed but in the co-ordinate of space-time. Specifically, what air transportation supposedly does is to transport a relatively high concentration of directed individuals to and from separate diaspora. In fact, it doesn't. Because the traveler is in a specific hurry, this much tells us already of trouble and demands a digression.

At the core of each problem there is a hard stone one calls "reality." That reality is of different degrees of gregariousness, depending on the degree of finality it subtends. The problem never has an adequate solution unless the real is programmed into the solution. The reality of the airport is highly gregarious because it is pseudo-instrumental, like a second-degree truth, like an artificial pearl. As it goes with parasitic organisms, the *causa prima* is outside of them. One can say that the airport is a parasitic appendix whose reason resides outside of itself precisely because the aim of the traveler is nowhere to be found inside of it.

My proposition is that we can, indeed we must, do without such an appendix. It is disproportionately greedy and disproportionately cumbersome. It is wrong in plan and location. My proposition is that the air terminal is to be assimilated or transformed into the city itself, the place where the traveler goes to and comes from.

It only partially matters that the actual situation calls for new airports serving old cities. Evolution does not find fit and propitious to persist on obsolescence. One falters in rationale if one deems as secondary the primary target of one's efforts. If I reach for an apple, the sponge I get instead is not for the well-being of me, the apple seeker. The traveler is evidently seeking anything but an airport in which he is and feels misplaced. The consequence of this misplacement we call frustration, disenchantment, fatigue, ruin, destruction, apocalypse according to where the consequences die. They seldom do die where we wish they would. A good example is the predicament man is in because of the car. In our case, the crux of the matter is, as it most often is, logistics.

Logistics in man is bodily and mental: transportation and communication. Giving communication to transportation in the micro-scale spectrum (electron-enzyme transfers) and setting it aside for the sake of the subject, air transportation, we have then to be imaginative enough (or have moved around enough) to see what transportation is when the digits (people and things) are not a few but are numberless . . . not one person going from one point of a diaspora to one point of another diaspora, but millions of people, hardware and things coming and going to and from different places: millions of them, and all moving to and from millions of places in the same compressed, liquefied time slot.

There is where the innocence of the speedy carrier, relatively effective in performance, thrusting through the air space, ends. The innocence of the air carrier is in its narrowly defined task of moving travelers, who have already grouped themselves in a specific spot where they will be bellied into the plane. When taken by itself, the price tag for this grouping is neatly swept under the rug. But the price tag is the airport, the parking lot, the freeway, the suburbias, the city itself. In a biological analogy we would be at a dead end. The biological organism cannot stand poor logistics. In fact, the biological organism is superb logistics. The society of man (in this case, the dislocated, disconnected, disturbed traveler) is, on the contrary, mired in poor logistics and stifled by it.

On the plane the passengers are homogenized for the common goal of the landing strip. There at the door of the plane the passenger re-emerges as his peculiar self, a self-directed speck among other self-directed specks, ill suffering any new and less efficient homogenization. His path is peculiar to himself. He has been transported. Now he is a traveler again, from the plane's door to the many places on his agenda. At this moment and point, time, distance and speed reassume their ordinary meaning. The hardware is slow or slowed down by the nature of the general configuration of the diaspora and the traveler's own peculiar goals, and speed is killed by uniqueness just as uniqueness is often killed by speed. But speed, the devourer of space, ill stands interruptions and distractions. In fact, where interruptions and distractions are introduced, such as stop signs, signals, traffic, bad roads, fog, rain, darkness, mechanical failure, dozing, recklessness, etc., speed is removed and cost skyrockets. (The light carriers and electricity carriers are the only privileged exceptions . . . in-

stant reach, 186,000 miles per second.) But we are bound
to the fact that acceleration and deceleration are demanding masters of velocity. Acceleration is also a gluttonous
monster and therefore a great pollutant. As soon as the
plane reaches the landing pad the passengers will no longer
be guests of her holy speed. They will collide myriads of
times with myriads of other moving and stationary bodies,
things, conditions, rules and taboos.

As distance can no longer be devoured by speed, time
and well-being must be saved in other ways. The only
way, the way constantly adopted by biological life, is the
contraction of space. Salvation is in those kinds of distances
that will cause acceptable humanly scaled time and fatigue gaps, the walking or semi-walking distance. There is
innocence refound. There is also the radicalization of the
urban structure, airport included. This new innocence is
as old as the first hiatus of life, two or three billion years
ago, when swiftness was discovered as synonymous with,
or at least indispensable to, life. But swiftness is only fitness. Or to be more precise, fitness is organized swiftness.
The swift traveler, not the hurried traveler, is the only
contented traveler. Then the relatively swift plane-passen-
ger configuration must not land itself into the semi-living
airport with its diaspora-monster of a problem—the city
included—yet not even acknowledged.

The truth of the matter is that we have an ebullient
propensity for adding bottlenecks inside of bottlenecks
and calling the result a product of affluence. On the subject in question, the primary bottlenecks are . . . the connection of the city to the airport, and the airport itself.
The secondary bottlenecks are . . . the ticket counter, the
luggage counter, and the door to the plane. Of these five
only the last one is necessary and acceptable. But the
ability to get rid of the other four is in the new innocence
suggested above. The new innocence, to use another
analogy, is when and where mankind's piece fits into the
puzzle of the cosmos. If man happens, and it would not be

by accident, to coincide with himself in the filia that "ought to be," then the puny problem of the airport will fuse itself into the problem of society with numberless others. If not, it will remain with man as one of the minor headaches of his confused species.

Before coming to the constructive part of my proposition, it might be well to face the concept of the usual and the unusual. If, by way of illustration, we cut open the body of an animal and observe, our confidence in what we call the usual or natural is shaken. It is a bloody congestion we watch there. Nothing polite or urbane about it. That is a hell of a creature twitching there, a universe furiously in pursuit, trying to survive, brutally single-minded, awesomely complex and secretive, indeed a most remote stranger to behold. And yet that is what we are, each of us, biological organisms. We are strangers to ourselves. What we know of what we are is literally skin-deep and our brainy contortions lodge somewhere out in the cold. We know but an abstraction of ourselves and we are despondently and disproportionately inclined to live by it. All this is to point out that the familiar proposition is not necessarily true and that the shock of revelation ought not by itself to alert one of the presence of the absurd. At a first glance, much that is not of our consciousness shocks as absurd and we are quick at rejection. It is almost as automatic as the biological rejection of a transplanted organ that we observe in medicine.

Into the urban body, I am conceptually introducing, and not too gently either, the city terminal, a semi-solid block of furiously driven events, a sanguine and animal turmoil covertly disciplined and multi-directed. The para-animal we call society falls under the rigor and the rules of the biological animal, for both are of the same universe and both the biological animal, achiever of incredible complexity, and society, oriented toward ever-increasing complexity, are complexity-driven.

A careful look at the nature of complexity will show

that it is, one might say, welded to the process of miniaturization. Complexity is an increment of co-ordinated
activities happening in contracting spaces. As there is no
complexification that does not coincidentally involve contraction, so there is no city without a corresponding miniaturization of the physical structure that supports it. It is
thus here where the new level of innocence bids farewell
to the romantic notion that man and soil (man and asphalt really) must mingle in an inexhaustible embrace.

Nature man and creator man, with all the cohorts of
middle and average man, are moving away from the soil
if hardly closer to that hypothetical kingdom of compassion and grace I like to call the esthetogenesis of matter. A
kingdom not in opposition to nature but constructing itself into a sur-nature. That is to say, that the nature of man
does not dwell in the guilded hamlets of home and gar-
dens, but it is thrust in that same unfamiliar and frightful
turbulence we discover inside the contented skin of all organisms. The contentedness reveals success, but success is
carried by an enormously rigorous discipline guided by
omnipresent rules. It is actually a miracle that perpetuates
itself, a triple miracle of consolidation, reiteration and
progression. Not, as one can see, the stuff suburbia and
megalopoly are made of, but the only stuff that can stand
and can spell the stresses of life's genesis.

The wandering away from the airport was not completely unintentional. Any analytical entanglement and
segregation is merciless, be it on the subject of air transportation, negative income tax or anything else. The case
of the airport is becoming a glaring example of insular
nonsense. Once purpose and instrumentality become in-
consequential, the solution is automatically out of sight.
It is instead historically right that once a technique, in
this case air transportation, has been proven as sound, it
be incorporated in the fabric of reality in the most coherent manner letting go of itself those parts that happen

to be of no more use. In the case of air transportation, the airport as an autonomous and physically isolated system has seen its day. If this is so, it has to go. The sooner the better. It is time we object to going nowhere and paying dearly for the going to it.

*We do not know how the complex works. We know that it is where life is, always. Then there is where life must be (next).*

# UTOPIA (Thoughts for the Steel Industry)

It is my belief that life is eminently a phenomenon of gathering and compressing matter-energy in peculiar ways. Selectivity is high in the gathering and organizing of the events composing the phenomenon. Selectivity becomes discrimination in the higher levels of the living process. What we witness is really the etherealization of nature at a pace which is defined by the evolutionary beat. But this process of etherealization is incapable of maintaining its pace whenever the mechanism that sustains it becomes inefficient. This mechanism is the already-mentioned gathering and organizing of matter-energy in events ever more interdependent, complex and highly organized in relatively diminishing spaces. This relative shrinkage or compression is not accidental or secondary; it is the only way by which the event can become more efficiently organized, that is to say, more impregnated with life. A cursory look at the behavior of matter-energy and at what is the play of information, communication, transportation in the living event explains why this is so. For life to be, it is necessary for the organism to be an enormously complex integration of right responses to an endless input of stimulae-informations.

In man, for the challenge-response cycles (millions at any given instant) to be right means to be specific, measured and timely. Specific as it has to deal with a unique situation; measured because only so does the specific become congruent to the case; timely because the flow of the process offers only one time slot for each response. If the "inertia load" of mass-energy and space-time is too great, the challenge-response cycle becomes defective and the organism suffers. If the ineffectiveness becomes endemic, the organism is crippled. If the ineffectiveness become epidemic, the organism is doomed. Most of our cities and towns are endemically afflicted, many are at an epidemic stage right now and are dying.

The reasons are not metaphysical. The enormously complex strand of events each one of us is finds itself in an utterly chaotic and unresponsive milieu, the city pseudo-structure. The ultra-sophisticated and sensitized phenomenon each of us is finds itself buried alive in a dungeon of insensitivity and impenetrability. Information and its communicability, knowledge and emotion sharing, physical transference of people and things . . . all those essential processes are mesmerized and curtailed. To do becomes a pain-filled undertaking, the inertial load; the space-time beats have become dumb to the vibrance of the comprehensive event. Congruence between the effort and the purpose has broken down; decay and desperation set in.

To foster the eventfulness of life, life itself has come up with a number of inventions, all of them designed ultimately for the selection of those physical media that will constitute the best support for the swifter ways of carrying information and fitting responses and for the most frugal ways to consume the energy that keeps the "machine" going. From the optimum conditioning of all those agencies, working together like an unbelievable clock, and after eons of "practicing," of struggle and self-sacrifice, life has come up with the fragile bud of self-determination, the free will. The unyielding discipline of the organism in all of its automatic performances is the only guaranty for the existence of free will, a condition necessary if not sufficient for its action.

What has this to do with the steel industry? Two things, at least.

1. Few if any actions of man upon raw nature have the demonic strength and the portentous skill of the process of gathering, selecting and compressing a certain amount of matter and physical properties out of the mega storage of the mineral crucible, as the actions of the steel industry have.

To take for granted the nail and the tanker, the spatula and the skyscraper, is part of the general failing of opulence. Metallurgy is one of those constant miracles of perseverance, foresight, planning and will, that are in a way too common nowadays to hold our fantasy and our awe. So if life and fulfillment are where the action is, gathering, selective, disciplined and powerful, one would expect them to be in the steel mill. Are they?

2. Is to make steel, those miracle metals, to foster automatically the life of a free agent, the person? The carnage of close to 60 million of those persons in the first half of the century, this literal annihilation of the future has had as prime tool and often as instigator (Krupp) steel and fire. If our stake in life is as reverential as the strength of the power we show in going about it, then we must soon see to it that our steel is made for life as reverently and passionately as a child's prayer. Science is not beyond morality; politics and nationalism are not beyond morality. They all are its servant or they all are evil. The whole technological world stares at us from the snake pit of our malice. But we are

sufficiently aware by now that the inner price of hypocrisy is outsmarting even the most callous of souls. If by
not other means than by the foul air he must breathe.

By making steel on specification, we know quite well
what will be its use. A count could or should be made of
the tonnage of steel, on one side of the scale, the tonnage
used for constructive purposes, on the other side of the
scale, the tonnage used for the gratification of our greed
and bigotry.

The steelmaker knows, by occupation, the complexity
inherent in any constructive process. If we put our attention to a specific process, the becoming of life, we
cannot but be struck by its awesome perfection, by its
inherent fragility, by its dependence on a balanced biosphere and by the all important fact that it can be fostered
only reverentially. If for nothing more than for human
self-preservation, the time has come for a choice between
unqualified corporate profit and becoming. They do not
coincide. They do not for the simple reason that life is not
free enterprise. It is instead a rigorous phenomenon, totally
tied to the larger mechanism of the universe. If our pride
is in producing the instrumentalities for life to develop
itself, we must also accept the stark facts of the human
logistics and of the human anguish. To serve the first, we
must wrap our action around the world in an uninterrupted
and strong net of co-ordinated performances designed for
man and for life. To serve the second, we must wrap such
a net in a peculiarly sensitized way, so as to let the
persons, soon 5 billion of us, puncture through and take
flight.

The radical contraction of instrumentality, the miniaturization of the man-made environment, will be the indispensable but not sufficient condition for the first. It will
take the family of man beyond survival into the blossoming of a terrestrial civilization, able, if willing, to take the
fluid sway of the myriad of free agents, the persons, into

a cultured world where the anguish of the species can atone into purpose.

First priority is the ethicalization of free enterprise, that is to say, the freeing of "free enterprise" from greed, hypocrisy, bigotry, fanaticism, intolerance. This is a task worth undertaking, to understate the case, and its challenge is far outdoing any other a corporate tycoon might accept.

Technology is not a neutral event. It is a soulless manifestation, supposedly harnessed by a soulful phenomenon. At every step technology must be given what it is not in its pristine condition to have. Technology is a loaded answer to the human condition. That explains why, for instance, the question of good and evil does not exist for the species not technologically proficient, why the law of the jungle, deprived of compassion as it is, is also incapable of malice. Innocence and technology part company at the outset and it is the constant responsibility of man to reconnect the two in bargaining his position among the other phenomena.

Technology would be neutral in a sense-less and passionless world. And if one wants to put an overdose of skepticism in postulating the possible, one could say that it is in the inertial guidance system of technology the intent of ridding reality of both senses and passion, so as to achieve "justness" and fitness. How far technology has succeeded in this direction is hard to conjecture. But to conjecture about it is important if we detect a general dulling and coarsening of man's sensitiveness. More things get lost by default than by intent as the passive condition is an ever-ready vacuum whenever initiative tapers away. Technology carries itself (and is reliable) because it is like a wound-up clock that will mark time, make time, regardless of what time is witnessing. Press on regardless is its strength and its nemesis, a nemesis that is totally negligible to "her" but fateful for man. Is there any guideline that can make sense out of what appears often to be a free-for-all melee? Some help can be found in the distinction between the practical and the real.

## THE PRACTICAL AND THE REAL

If I were to say that I will be guided in my action by what I deem practical, I would really say nothing at all. To say something significant one should say: In my action I will be guided by what I consider practical within a certain context, a context made of time, space, ancestry, social and cultural milieu, sentiment, environment, ecology . . . once we put the practical action within a sufficiently large context, the practical coincides with the real. If and when we put it in a quasi-obliterated context, a context limited to the immediate, the practical coincides with the irresponsible, with the utopian (the non-place), the unreal. Why is this so?

It is so because there are no phenomena that are not spatially, temporally and psychomentally far larger than what they might appear at first. It is in ourselves that we see this affirmed. In an endless stream, through us and by us individuals, comes to pass the texture itself of the human phenomenon. Mentally, emotionally, existentially, we are permanently "cantilevered out" pervading spherically as large zones of influence as the strength of our minds and our souls can afford. To shrink within the boundaries of our physical skin is literally to shrivel and die.

In a less metaphysical or private realm, we have had also some striking examples recently: the omnipresence of DDT and its consequence, the deadly dynamic of war psychosis and the resulting savagery, or closer to the neighborhood scene, the Jones's complex or the hippy complex. . . . We, the software of reality, and any and all of the things we have produced and overproduced are only the center of a certain performance whose resonance is ever penetrating larger and larger spheres in time and space. There is thus a space perspective and a time perspective which are a non-dismissable part of our pragmatism. The more we cut away from them and disregard, the weaker is our participatory position in the making of the present. As knowledge is the sense of perspective, it is then quite right that knowledge has the ability to discover more and more deficiencies within the sphere of the practical. That is to say, knowledge introduces greater and greater obsolescence into those things that are not sufficiently part of the general staging of the present, to the point where the practical event becomes senseless. It has been overridden by reality. Some examples . . .

The practical farmer moves from one acreage to the next, exhausting the soil at each installment and setting the stage for ecological disaster.

The real farmer measures his conduct so as to care for the balanced interaction of his doing and the doing of nature.

Practical man sees in uniformity, unblemishedness, "sterilization" and packaging the marketability of foodstuffs . . . Real man knows that the real value of foodstuffs is not to be found there at all. Indeed, he knows that such marketing devices are fundamentally unhealthy, wasteful, pollutant and fraudulent.

Practical man thinks nothing of driving ten miles to get a carton of beer . . . Real man knows that out of billions and billions of such trips, day in, day out, the earth is becoming less livable, the sky becomes less and less and less clear, the seas less and less healthy, the energy sources of the earth are depleted, nations are at each others throats, etc., etc.

Practical man does his own things in the name of and under the cover of free enterprise . . . Real man knows that man cannot do his own things for the elementary reason that his own things are everybody's things, that

the private and the public or collective are totally en-
meshed and inextricably bound by a common destiny.

Practical man takes Bufferin for the body and for the
soul to the point of dumbness . . . Real man takes pain
to see where he steps in, even when the step is painful.

Practical man takes consent at face value and gets
politically in the seat of power . . . Real man sees history
as an endless denunciation of opportunism and stands or
falls on its own merits.

Practical man wins all battles and loses all wars . . .
Real man views tactics as the instruments of strategy.

The American practical man, after winning so many
battles, is in the throes of defeat. Indochina is a literal
example of abstract men doing the practical thing, brutalizing themselves, devastating a country, mesmerizing
life, ending up with a handful of bloody feathers and a
criminal record. The list can fill a volume because we all
act most of the time as practical-utopian individuals.

## THE PLUMBER OF UTOPIA

For every man the sphere of the real has a different
capacity. The plumber is acting in a real context up to
the point where his mind is oriented toward the well-
working of a faucet. The plumber-scholar is not real man
even if he can still do a good job at plumbing. He is not
real-man because he knows better, he knows that more
"beautiful" plumbing is subordinated to a better condition
of grace for all men, but he will not accept the challenge
of his knowledge. For him the practical and the real do
not frame each other. The vast canopy of reality is concealed by the puny umbrella of practicality. In a very
"real" way most of us are spoiled plumbers. We know inside ourselves that reality is a burning fire, but we choose
to steal away crumbs of life, and "Praise the Lord" for
that.

The spoiling knowledge does of our practicality is the
way life has of discarding worn-out paradigms. As the

pace of change rushes upon us more new things in shorter times, the rate of obsolescence is on a constant increase. A consequence of this is that unless we frame larger and larger perspectives of the past to guide us into the future, we become less and less apt to come up with contextual responses. That means the widening of the gap between the practical in the purely present tense and reality as such. The more we go about constructing analytical responses in the naked present, the more such responses become irrelevant to the corposity of the dilemmas of life.

The reasons for our shortsightedness are multiple. At times it is pure greed, at times it is piety, at times it is anything in between them. For the greedy and the parasite even long planning is only a one-dimensional structure whose context is the blind alley of fear, survival and power. On the opposite end, the pious soul, feeding the hungry, sheltering the pauper, has the context of his responses consumed in the vise of desperation, brotherly but hopeless. In his existential piety he forgoes the more demanding axiality of compassion. The context of reality has to be a fully developed phenomenon, for which, in a way, even greed might be atoned by vision (the Maecenate—patron) and piety resolve itself in the fire of compassion. This entails for both extremes and for the various degrees in between, perspectives and learning going, by reason of self-fulfillment, beyond the thin, weak and blind ongoing of practicality.

Mind you, this pauperism in substance often produces enormous physical thrusts as the market inundated by futilities demonstrates. But those tides flushing the landscape of today's society are inherently sterile and, contrary to the fecundity brought in by the mud of the Nile, what they leave behind is waste and garbage in a typically modern and ecologically open cycle, smoldering with the blessing of pollution.

It is not idle to ponder how far practical man has

mastered the development of this country and what heritage he is putting in the hands of the generations to come. It is an open question how a doer tycoon like Henry Ford would judge a managerial tycoon or a corporate steamroller. Henry Ford was a realist in as much as he went about making mobile a relatively simple and tenuously distributed society, the society of his day. The Fords of today are practical men working into the abstract, utopian non-world of suburbia. They are disconnected from reality, which is a far more encompassing and pervasive universe than the one they are bent upon. It was a real achievement for Henry Ford to give man a marvelous toy to play with. It is a savage accomplishment for Detroit to foster and feed a perverse state of affairs where an incredible amount of wealth, knowledge, toil and energy of the whole earth are literally burnt on the altar of mobility (where and when mobility is still the end-product). The same can be said for the pharmaceutical, the food, the sport, the games and the respectability markets. By bunching in one bundle the feasible and the desirable, we have become amoral and hypocritical. This has been called the morality of the dollar. It is very much the morality of the practical man, once we carry the investigation into the often well meaning origin of the process. This does not speak well of naïveté and ignorance; it rather denounces them as the origin of evil when the context is a complex, problematic, unpredictable society. Good intentions feed the dragon as well and as much as the bloody malice. Which presents us with the triple problem of knowledge, action and vision, as only by them together can we operate under the canopy of reality. Big deal, you can say, this is a truism. The gain is that the real has been unhinged from the fraudulence of the practical mind. We always and only get what we ask for. To make things short it is up to us to choose stagnation and breakdown or growth and evolution.

## THE FEASIBLE, THE DESIRABLE

Practical man, the plumber, up and down the ladder of action must bring himself to his senses before nemesis does the job for him and all. He must take the feasible to the laboratory where feasibility is checked by desirability and where feasibility-marketability have no voice unless they clearly show unequivocal desirability. It is most feasible and most profitable in marketing terms to produce an endless chain of ingenious gadgets, one making the other necessary. Any department store overflows with this sort of thing. In the light of the massiveness of the phenomenon, the validity and justifiability of so much ingenuity, so much toil, so much mass-energy-depletion are questionable. We must remember that opulence is not only the privilege of parasitism. It is also the *deux ex machina* of waste, destruction, pollution and envy, segregation and bigotry. Let's do first what is needed, then what is valid and fulfilling and let extravagance be a minor fringe of our action. This is the least we can give as a contribution to the miracle of life.

But to do what is necessary escapes practical man as he is given to brick laying, not to the conceiving and defining of the wall, and the wall is endless and ubiquitous. It is recognizable only at a distance by sharpened vision, and from deep concern and proven "authority." From this absence of "vision" comes the other grand illusion that we can as individuals design our communities. As we, persons of different training, cannot design but a small percentage of all the things we use and misuse, so we, as non-specifically trained "planners," cannot assume the task of conceiving and constructing beyond the limits of our private life. The only way we can imprint ourselves into the physical environment is if we are somehow in the favorable position of being offered a global-physical context that is amenable to our needs and that can move us and require from us personal involvement in our immediate surrounding (home or occupational place).

This presupposes a structure and a discipline in the large environmental context which is negated now by the quicksand of chaos, squalor, confusion, license, atomization. This points at the other failings of practical man that I have pointed out before. He does not take hold of the fact that to be a free agent is inherently conditioned by the tyranny of the living condition. The biological phenomenon is a routinized, automatized miracle where the discipline and co-ordination is utterly rigorous and unforgiving. It is on such reliable foundations that the free will has a chance to develop. But as this new dimension of the evolutionary process is somehow instituting its ever-new instrumentalities at its own level, such instrumentality must be analogous in rigor and structural soundness to the biological instrumentalities free determination operates on, when the social context is evolutionary. The utopian character of the practical world is just this non-evolving, nowhere, non-place, within which practical man operates. The non-place of disconnection, confusion, senselessness, despair and numbness which practical man has constructed around himself. If only I could grasp it, he says, then I could make sense of my doing. But it is his own doing that obliterates the thing he vainly seeks to grasp. There is nothing to grasp there but the failure of an endeavor warped by the lack of spirit and hope. As practical man operates now, he is the least free of us all.

I would suggest that the creation of a new urban environment demands the upgrading of practical man into real man. It is the opening of the most fantastic new market any industry can wish for. Will we move into it inside the hide of a tyrannosaurus rex, fangs dripping blood, brain cast in an osseous prison, mind cluttered by the poison of voracity, or are we going to enter it humanly, consciously, discriminately, reverently? The whole earth, her lands, her seas, her forests and animals, her sky and rivers, her people, her children are all partaking in the same vigil. To fail her with the mastery of power we now act with is possibly to fail her without appeal. Time is an irreversible event and time runs out; it does. Where and how can we realistically cope with the ever mounting demands of complexifying life?

# ARCOMEDIA

1. The visual and the audio are an extraordinary part of the contemporary world, and they partake both of high sophistication and dismal grossness. The sophistication is the outcome of demand and market pressures on a background of technical inventiveness. The grossness is part fad, part unmitigated naïveté and ignorance.
2. Both visual and audio have not been fully deployed on scale and impact, if not under restrictive and primitive conditions (Woodstock, etc.).
3. Many of the most recent applications (lasers, holograms, etc.) are just now beginning to enter the market.
4. The high responses elicited from audiences and viewers, even by raw experiments, indicate a limitless potential market for bold and novel applications.
5. The sun, the moon and the stars have not been considered as resources in the audio-visual-sensorial spectrum. They are indeed the most impressive of all and the role they should play is to be considered. This brings in cosmographic, geographic, climatologic and

morphologic elements and a practically endless combination of the media by themselves and within the environmental context.

Some relationships between man and a media-orientated environment:

1. The sun and the structure
2. The sun and the performance
3. The night and the structure
4. The night and the performance
5. The light of man
6. The sound of man
7. Research and experimentation
8. Performances and festivals

The structure, an arcology capable of about 3,000 inhabitants, is a large instrument for investigation and performance in the multimedia field that would take constant and attentive stock of the originating elements of nature. Linear investigation on light, sound, taste, smell, skin sensitivity would flow into the multilinear and simultaneous event. Participating in the performance would be the specific technical devices developed by the audio-visual-sensorial technology plugged in, so to speak, to the environment, people and building included. The spectator would be pulled in by the unpredictability, the magnitude, the power of the images, the sounds, the structures, the spaces, the dynamics and synchronization of the performances and by the amount of information of synthetic-environmental kind implied by them. A series of centers of attention and centers of action would come to life according to programmed schedules throughout the structure, the spaces, walls, floors, roofs, etc. Suddenly or gradually the landscape itself would be called into the performance, with it the specific manifestations of ecological, geological, biological, seasonal, historical and chronological kind. Then the cosmological elements of sun, moon, stars, radiations, magnetic fields, space . . . through transference, reflection, refraction, enlargement, triggering, concentration, collection, response, reaction, etc. Then with them the intervention of the esthetic: music, poetry, "fine arts," cinema, dance, mimicry, etc. . . . pageantry, rituals . . . Stress must be put in the contrast between the documentation by the various media of what nature is and does and the specifically created grace of which man is the originator. Though we all know that the experimentator or the documentator will always imprint the document with his own personal plea, we also know that there is something of a chasm between the registration of a natural event and a play of a Molière or an Ionesco.

The more we can grasp of the ways of nature, the more we will be able to gauge the enormity of our responsibility. We really move from innocence to responsibility, from the innocence of the vegetal and animal life to the responsibility of the human mind. Both have to contend for their life with the physical and energetic universe.

## NORMATIVE CONCEPT
Environmental information versus synthetic information.

The more we are shifting our teaching methods from the teacher-empiricisms-pupil base, the more we face the specter of the naked mind. By the naked mind I mean that mind which has been saturated with indirect information and has been deprived of personal experience. For instance, there are two ways to teach an infant about hot and cold. One is to present to him images of events occurring in a hot surrounding, beads of sweat covering the face of a workman, and images of events occurring in a cold surrounding, an Eskimo child bundled in its fur coat. The other is to take his hand and put it under a water faucet, turn first the hot water on, then the cold. For the first child the knowledge of hot-cold will remain in the visual context of abstractions and symbols. For the second, it will be a personal sensation, physically experienced and directly connected with the categories of adaptability and survival.

The accumulation of thousands of bits of abstract information in the brain of the first child, information which is not introduced perceptually by the senses to which the sensation belongs, but introduced directly into the mind by the symbolic apparatuses of sounds (words) and sights (images), will tend to disjoint the activity of his brain from the action of his body. The mind will thus tend to work out responses on a similar level of abstraction. It will, for instance, find it less difficult to induce the body to pull the lever showering napalm on strangers (here there is also a second level of abstraction in the spatial remoteness of the consequence, a third level in the patriotic cover motivating the crime). The naked mind is thus a sophisticated version of the savage mind. The sophistication comes from the impressive sphere of abstract information the brain has in store and is ready to pull out to explain and rationalize the behavior of the person it presides over.

The abstract or naked mind is more difficult to deal with than the "sinful" mind because it is not guilt ridden but amoral. Its goals are often experimentation (in a savage twist of experience deprivation) and puzzle solving that generate social, political, cultural and ethical crises. It is not necessary for the naked mind to go as far as the brutal, it is quite enough for it to deal inappropriately with the routine of life. The general desensitizing of the person, body and mind, coupled with an "explosive" pressure of the intelligence working out schemes of action based on a wealth of synthetic information, generates an intellectual pollution far more deadly than the physical cloud blanketing the earth. It is indeed responsible for it, as there is nothing like the ability of the naked mind to do well the wrong thing. That causes more irrelevance and, as direct consequence, waste. In fact the naked mind is compelled by its own standard of perception and by the abundance of its information into frenzies of feasibility. As feasibility is made speculatively rewarding by the ethos of advertising-consumerism, feasibility becomes a criteria for desirability. To the naked mind this is a sufficient and necessary reason for action. The gluttony of the production-consumption carnival is the result. Thus we have (a) squalor as the end product of a wealthy society, (b) the social and cultural pauperism derivated from (c) the enormous wastefulness of a chronically sick priority scale.

## THE NAKED MIND AND TECHNOLOGY

The danger presented to man by the multimedia is in the "empathy" of the technology for the norms of the naked mind, the mind not environmentally mature. If information is defined not as the accumulation of data, but as the combined data perception, the weight of the emotive appropriation of it and the subsequent interwelding between the "hot" data occurring in the mind, one can say that there is a certain inherent dosage of information the brain can accept to assure a relative ability for context and for moral decisions. The naked mind will store a greater number of (naked or cold) bits of information as those are less cumbersome, simpler, not yet fraught by the fogs of doubt. And, what is most telling, they have not flared up at the contact of what has received them. They have not become knowledge. This describes the mode of the computer; in fact, that is what the purely naked mind is best comparable to.

The environmental information appeals more to the person, flesh, blood and soul, as it is information directly touching the biopsychological organism and comes to it within a non-remote context (the hand feeling temperature instead of the mind getting a symbolic notion of it).

As it is sooner or later demanded from each individual

to engage in (abstract) organization of thoughts, it is
enormously important that at the base of the pyramid of
mental construction, on the strength of which action comes
about, there be as rich as is circumstantially possible a collection of concrete perceptions to which the abstract no-
tions can be gauged (hence the access from the planned
to the acted) while guarding itself from the ruthless
dictum of means justifying ends or the password of the
pure segregated efficiency of practical man. In a way,
the greater the power of abstraction of the mind is, the
more the body should have been previously trained and
sensitized. *Mens sana in corpore sano* where sanity is
primarily a fine tuning on what the real is doing. At the
opposite end of the scale is the not too farfetched case of a
newborn baby boxed into an information machine and
developed remotely from the vagaries of flesh and emotions into a stupendous and steely machine for thinking
—whose thinking cannot, by circumstantial "upbringing,"
include but the purely mathematical relationship of cause-
effect in the absolute indifference toward good and evil.

The environmental mind can cope with a lessened number of digits because the digits it deals with are by themselves composite of a pure nucleus, the data, and of all the
fringes and strands attached to it by the sensitized organism that hosts them. Then the apprehension of the
same event, birth or death for instance, is imprinted on the
brain in as many ways as there are circumstantial sets of
apprehension. We go then from the cold description of the
fanatic analyst on one extreme to the participatory context of the poet on the other. From the clean full color
wide screen documentation to the fully contextual trauma
of the non-mediated, personal witnessing. One thousand
deaths on the TV screen are "not worth" one real touch-
able death. Which is why, by the way, killing becomes far
easier for the TV watcher than for the occasional butcher.

In Arcomedia I am attempting to reconnect the naked

mind to the body. I do so by linking the audio-visual to the physical universe expressed by the environment and by compelling the spectator, not into doing his own thing, which he can do on other occasions, but into being invested by visual and acoustic phenomena of traceable contextual and existential nature: the ongoing of nature around and within ourselves. For instance, that the sun is a formidable furnace is common knowledge, but uncommon feeling. To convey an indelible impression about this monstrous machine, whose remote energy can caress us or burn us into a crisp, is of prime importance for the normative premises of a cultured person. That on the earth of cooled-down matter a not less formidable fire is to be kindled by the immensely secretive phenomenon of life is also part of a normative platform for action. Therefore, the importance of a correlated event expressing the linkage between physio-chemical fire and biomental fire within the evolutionary journey must be realized. This kind of experience is a must if we want to insert the phenomenon of life in the universal context.

# THE AMERICAN WITHDRAWAL
# FROM AMERICA

The difference between the complex and the complicated is that the first hungers for ever more "richness"; the second is in desperate need of simplification. The stricken metropoly, the Gordian Knot of complicated drives and breaking-down machinery, attempts survival by diffusing itself through explosion into the "simplified" suburbia. In contrast, the lively community, by the momentum of its intensity, is pushed from within to an ever more subtle co-ordination of things, a more complex milieu. From the complicatedness of the sick metropoly to the torpor of suburbia is to go from bad to worse, unless the suburban phenomenon is only a quarantine station expectant of a new beginning toward a vigorous social and cultural environment. The house (city) has to be abandoned from time to time for disinfestation and renovation and yet it is also necessary that the return be swift and determinate. We are not abandoning the cities, we are temporarily leaving them because they need reconception and regeneration. In this light, the urbanite who be-

comes the suburbanite, beats to the punch the do-gooder,
the social and political workhorse, the planner, who are
after survival by the domino theory in reverse. A little
good here, a little good there and the house will re-
furbish itself by the miracle of seepage, of goodness into
badness, which is exactly the reverse of what is in reality
happening: the conversion of the little gracile goodness
into unmitigated badness by the laws of assimilation of the
less forceful by the more forceful. This honest and pious
toil pales in the harsh light and the unintended compassion of the involuntary revolutionary tearing himself, his
family, his work away from the city. Fear and frustration
are the lubricant of his exodus. This *après moi le déluge*
of a gigantic crowd of little despots bent on a quasi-
genetic mutation will see the cities go to dust so as to set
the stage once more for the myth of the phoenix.

This leaving is more radical than the purely physical
tearing away from one's environment and resettling else-
where. It involves also the sacrifice of those things which
are not capable of being lifted to another place. Those
things are the spirit of the city and the intense social-
cultural-ethic articulations grown in the city by its not
purely metaphysical presence. It is perhaps less coherent
than curious that a technically oriented society will adopt
the oversimplifying techniques of technology to "solve" its
paradoxes and come up with the oversimplification of
sub-urbia. This reliance on the hidden paradigm of technology stipulating that it is only necessary to peel one leaf
at a time in order to get hold of the core, as if reality
were a simple onion, is the deterministic prison of western
man. Such ethos gives heart to the exodus. The fact is that
the American society is withdrawing from itself. It is a
massive withdrawal that consigns the job of information
and communication to radio, television and the logistics
of survival and surfeit to the automobile. Electricity, elec-
tronics, rubber, pistons, oil, cement and asphalt are the

mythical *deus ex machina* of withdrawal. Furthermore, as the exodus is massive and selective at the same time, the 80 per cent of the white middle class purged of the 20 per cent minority poor, the withdrawal is frightfully utopian. Therefore it is in for a tidal reversal toward a centered biospherically coherent rebirth of the civitas. But what is more, it is naturally utopian inasmuch as it is counter to the spiraling of life toward translife. This double utopianism in the withdrawal of a whole society is the most impressive force of revolution by default. It is the classic example of the forming of a vacuum that, abhorred by nature, and life in it, will inevitably become the stage of one of the most cyclonic series of centers, the eye of the hurricane of the spirit, the "civitate dei" of the next millennium.

## THE REVOLUTIONISTS

Then, if the suburbanite cannot be called the most revolutionary force in the United States (this would imply greater consciousness of one's historical significance), he can definitely be the most revolutionizing. He has, in addition, the hand on the production-consumption throttle. He is, thus, the maker or the breaker of civilization and is one of the myriads forcing the country into withdrawal, the present phase of the American phenomenon. This is, in itself, a sufficient reason why the American scene is the most ripe of all for the radicalization of the environment with the birth of the arcological era and all the implications it contains.

Diagrammatically, one can put the evolutionary spiral in its two dimensional projection this way:

1. Origin of the urban nodule as a magnet of life.
2. Complexification of it into the city and its aims.
3. The deterioration of the city by way of the complicated machinery of expediency, loss of aim by decomplexification.

4. The urban environment becomes the antithesis of its purpose; it becomes anti-human.
5. The city decomplexifies itself into sub-urbia in the attempt of ridding society and its environment of the complicated (wasteful) machineries, functional gigantism and bureaucracy.
6. The city becomes a functional, social, cultural vacuum surrounded by a mobile and yet ossified, withdrawn society (the present moment).
7. A quasi-physical tension causes a wind of centration of society into arcological systems. Society returns from its withdrawal.

EVOLUTIONARY SPIRAL

If this phasing repeats itself, it can free itself from the cyclical root only if spirally surging upward so as to never retrace its path twice. In this light, the suburbia of today might contain more vital force, knowledge and trust than the little communities of yesterday. This is only possible if such suburbia is also more complex than those small communities.

Could it be valid to reverse the concept and say that the opposite is true? That the cities, centers of withdrawal of a society that has urbanized itself in the short span of two generations, have burst like swollen bags, letting the citizenry return to the land and the innocence of their ancestors? Hardly. Unless withdrawal stands for the opposite of what it is. One does not withdraw into the storm nor does one seek a reappraisal of one's self by an inversion in the currents of life that most likely have triggered the desire or the need for self-examination. Nor is the psychosomatic reaction of withdrawal (like the snail retracting its dendrils and itself in its mobile home which is immobilized in the trailer park) a reaction that will make one walk into the bins of boiling water because of fear and distrust.

One withdraws from intensity, not into it, as one withdraws from conditions which bottom in the dread for death. Death is not a place for withdrawal but a place to return from, if that were at all possible. Both great blinding events and decay and naught are the sponsors of withdrawal. Suburbia is a place for quiescence, for non-action, and stands suspended within the storm tearing away between intensity and naught. The holy man withdrew from the corrupted Sodoms into caves or up columns. The affluent man withdraws from the Gomorrahs to the padded "comfort" of the suburban home. They both seek something better from life. Neither of them can be contradicted if the appraisal is a one-take shot. How mystifying this flat prospective is explains how utopian, naught, the thing itself is. Unless perspective is given to this "thing" the corposity of the phenomenon leaves the premises of the present and any change, no matter how grim, is called progress.

Unlimited withdrawal, the prospective taken away from the future, is unlimited renunciation as it signifies that the challenge of intensity has been shut away and not responded to. Once the withdrawal has permitted the reorientation of one's own posture, one might find that the element missing in suburbia is the intellectual pressure that has driven the saint into a withdrawal poised as a steppingstone for etherealization. The withdrawn suburbanite strikes one as a step in the other direction. There the steppingstone becomes the tabernacle well stocked for hibernation and desensitization. The connectors of TV and radio, linking it to the world by striking the chords of fear and discomfort into the well-fed if not sullen body, might not for a while at least reawaken a conscience but make it burrow ever more so in the cracks of isolation and self-reassurance. Comfort and "well-being" (physical, that is) discourage risk, adventure and self-examination. They are embalmers unless the spirit is unremittingly at work, which is that condition that tends to keep those same comforts, and physical well-being, out of the house in the first place. What will make the withdrawal temporary and fruitful will be the human conscience. The intellect can betray man more easily than his conscience. Ultimately man will burrow out of his prison not because of a crystalline vision of a new era but because his soul will literally throw him out of the cocoons of the ego. We witness such things right now. As it mostly happens by the channels of the offspring, its validity is marred by the absence of direct personal cost. The child finds it far easier to give away the basketful of apples than the parents who have gone through the often agonizing process of producing the basketful. A more realistic assessment of the sins of the fathers (and mothers) is that they are a murky assemblage of shortcomings, more than either the few blemishes on candid snow of selflessness many of them pretend or the black tar of evil many of the sons and daughters are so delirious about. But the generosity of ignorance of sons and daughters can be only a fleeting blessing if the momentum of it is not stronger than the impetus closing the gap between abundance and dereliction (the living on the spin-offs from the opulent society). And the deprived are not by disposition the good samaritans. Survival does not imply a holy disposition, just a frugal one, inasmuch as greed is still beyond one's own means or plans.

## KNOWLEDGE

The return from withdrawal implies the reappearance of a richer self ready to give of its own to man, as a dividend of one's own growth. If the return is another escape, one among the many, it is a pretty sterile act among others.

American society is withdrawing from itself. It is a massive migration away from the centers that were being formed by the urbanization of rural America. The first impression is of unbound dynamism, a whole society quivering and flowing as if a hundred volcanoes had gone into operation erupting flesh, minds and homo faber—magical worlds perpetually aglow and smoldering. The deception that conceals the massiveness of it all is distance, separation and isolation, that same isolation that is at the end of the tunnel and obscures to their participant their participatory sorcery. And if dynamism is to be gauged by energy transfer (consumption) and degradation, dynamic is the process, gargantually so, bewilderingly so . . . parasitically so, unfortunately. Volcanism and holism do not meet in most cases and the dynamics of holism, the unerringly centered phenomenon of life, is not measurable by energy consumption but by how much of this physical energy reappears in the subtler, metamorphosed form of energy of the spirit. The furnace is justified by the warmth of the house.

One can observe three distinct waves. One wave, now waning, is the migration from the land into the towns and cities. Jobs and options of life modes through learning and civic institutions were the driving forces. Another is the exodus from towns and cities toward the suburban diaspora; comfort, "simplicity," "nature's setting," "independence," the deceiving goals. A third wave is the ever-moving of one third or so of the population from job to job, from mirage to mirage, from novelty to more of the same, motivated by necessity (job market), by uprootedness, by curiosity, by instability, by lack of self-discipline. The true symbol of this ubiquitously peripatetic fraction of humanity is the mobile home and the trailer court. Never mind that the one, or two, or three sets of wheels under the floor could well be in cardboard as the house is very seldom rolling. The fact is that the tenants are, and the rolling stock under the floor gives them the comfortable feeling of flight on a moment's notice. Even if and when the house expands around the aluminum core into bricks and stones, pots and plastic chairs, the flame is kept burning and Mercury is still postured on the edge of his seat, ready for flight, unmindful of the empty socket that might be left behind.

As the second and third waves are the thing of the moment, what really is being acted is the withdrawal of an entire nation from itself. Such a large phenomenon is going to produce tensions of cataclysmic intensity. We are feeling now just the first premonitory shakes and they already are leaving politicians, economists and planners out of breath and half-witted. The belly of society has given away and no amount of deodorant can conceal for long the unpleasant odors of the half-digested social and civil proteins thrusted out into the air already saturated with the bigger and smaller-than-filters techno-dollar particles.

The pendulum swings so far out and up and with such a ponderous load of attributes, one thing of everything for every man, woman, child and pet and with such dread of soulfulness, that it is the most kinetic of all swords of Damocles. It will return hurricanelike in force to "pressurize" society in the psychosomatic phalansteries of a reborn society, or it will put to fire and fury the whole continent. Of this return the first coagulations are the communes ever so innocently sold as the "Garden of Eden Year 2000," not in Sears or NASA catalogues but in the earth catalogues and in the tender folds, butterfly brains of the flower children. Swept away or unrecognizable after the first assault of the underhumanized suburbanites, they will have sounded for the last time the simplistic ways of a nature, original in pristine times, now out of synchrony with its own soul, man. The uncomplicated commune dwellers and the undercomplex suburbanites; one group laboring for a Christian-communism electronically rocking, the other waspishly capitalistic and electronically automatized will curse innocence so bewitching in their pets, so fraudulent in their souls and, faced by the naught of isolation, will turn to the complex phenomenology of cooperative and instrumentalized life, the whole three, four, five or who knows how many billions of us making it.

# JOY AND ANGUISH IN THE LUST BAG (Fragments for a Doctrine)

It might be that of all acts, bar none, the orgasm is that intense event in which the two most telling characters of the humane—playfulness and anguish—fuse more into one, and do so on the bridge of organic life. This fusion has a lot to do in making the orgasm a uniquely sensitized condition, which is somewhat as metaphysically pregnant as physiologically pregnant the act might be.

The exuberance of the body which makes for playfulness is like a thread guiding male and female on the edge of existence and at his stronger best gives them in one sole paroxysm the physiological thrust and a mental glance into naught. As if consciousness were to pull itself from under the I and the Thou, and do it there at the peak of joy, leaving them prey to forces to which they do not belong. As if to say, "Here, see, even at your sublime best, the chasm of naught engulfs you."

It would seem, then, that life makes use of the sexual urge as the device by which to surprise man, the playful animal, with a sudden tide of anguish, a catastrophic catharsis. While the body is run through by something that has driven away playfulness and brought in fury, the fist that such fury shakes at the gods turns into a gesture of terror and a plea. There, at that instant, one is emptied and made useless: one becomes the disposable receptacle. Then one dies (Dionysus) as often as one copulates and, in the dissipation of the moment, the female is the receptacle of a shattered being, as well as the mooring of his semen. Consummation is in this realm a very appropriate word because, at least for the male, something inside is "given up" psychologically as well as physiologically.

In the unconsumed orgasm, the wretched Christ finds receptacle in the body of the mystic priestess and, fueled by the burning semen of the body, the flame of His soul shrouds her. By this fiery turnout, joy and anguish fuse to compound the food, the energy, the light for the mind of man. There Civitate Dei is the mystic priestess, aflame by the burning of man-Christ as His playfulness flashes against the massive wall of anguish and precipitates the esthetogenetic metamorphosis.

This metamorphosis is the novel quantum that, unable to create itself through the orgasm of the body and the biological conception, bursts into being as etherealized emergence into the orgasm of the mind. It is the emergency of the occasion which is made into the emergence of the spirit. Emergency is often the catalyst or the trigger for the emergence of a new consciousness. Friendship, tenderness, love that might never surface between two persons who hide themselves under a shield of banalities, will do so through the opening made by some condition or emergency. This condition is not limited to physical or psychological traumas of a negative nature, but can be more promisingly of a cultural-social kind. By rubbing raw in one spot the tough skin of self-defense, the trauma-emergency exposes, as in metal welding, as much of the pure metal as to let the heat of the situation fuse one to the other. A poem, a play, a movie, a cityscape, a reading, powerfully charged, can make for the encounter. This emergence, by the mediatory presence of the cultural event for which the institutions of knowledge and culture are necessary, might never come about, but it does when the conditions of emergency have adequate instruments themselves with which to make possible the emergence into grace. The instruments and mediator are in this case extra-personal, cultural. In the orgasm there is somehow both the condition of emergency and the ferments of emergence. The dilemma is that those ferments are most active the closer one is to the final blow, but still on this side of it, before it.

In some way then, the orgasm is an abortive creation where the emptiness of the aftermath is the physiological counterpoint of a moment creatively astray. In other words, in the orgasm are two of the three ingredients of esthetogenesis: joy, anguish and vision, where vision has been played down by playfulness which is at the end to be the surprised companion of anguish.

As vision and playfulness are somewhat related (they both transcend the rational), some degree of creation rubs into the orgasm as some orgasmlike fluttering is in the creative act.

Furthermore, anguish, to be conscious of itself, must hide within its sullen body fragments of joy as only in one's own opposite one finds the true deprivation of one's condition. Anguish is otherwise, in its pure inalterability, desperation.

"Joyless" anguish is the black hole of desperation into which life falls to become once more the dumbness and unconsciousness of matter-energy. "Joyful" anguish is the "necessity" of taking that same universe of matter-energy as both the media and the subject for the esthetogenesis of the becoming. In as much as fear is part of the situation, fear can be seen as the objectification of anguish; if so, one can find its resolution by caging away the object. When the object is too large for any cage, fear becomes an immanent resident of the subject. It is anguish, then, because in such cases the confrontation is between the living and all that which the living sees as his own nemesis. For this state of things, running away is to run in denser folds of such nemesis. The resolution is genesis, the puncturing by anguish of the deterministic mega-bag of the universe and the blossoming on it, around it, and finally in it of the esthetocompassionate universe of the spirit. This is why fear is sterile while anguish is fertile. When the consciousness of joy germinates within anguish, the compassionate takes hold there, from orgasm on one side and creation on the other.

As one is deprived when one is one half of the human animal, it is expected that in the absence of the physiological "resolution," the individual will attempt on his own the "stunt" of creation and succeed at times to transcreate by leaping beyond the organic. But the presence of both anguish and joy must furnish the compassionate context. Vision is the structure which, fertilized by the compassionate, will germinate with the creative act.

Vision is the non-necessary ingredient of orgasm, but when present will make of it both a more intense experience and a more pain-filled one.

The envelope and the carriage of these elements is lust— the organic hunger swaying on its surges and intellectual indifference, the body and the psyche.

If lust is a bag, empty of compassion and also deprived of vision, then animality is all that is there to wrest out. If vision is in, in its lonely self, it is then like a clinical operation carried furiously to its conclusion on the barren rocks of disconnection and finally disgust. Vision does not survive a "purely" intellectualized orgasm. It will shatter and take in its downfall the soul which anyhow had been in the betrayal from the beginning.

It goes without saying that the esthetic act does not necessitate the lustful bag for its advent, though it might be that such a container had a placental function at the origin of man's history.

The lust bag contains also a heterogeneous assemblage of things: the aggressiveness of the hunter, the protectiveness of the male, his possessiveness, the body counter, the adventurer, the mocker, and the female things somehow symmetrically disposed. In far less attractive cases, the sadist, the raper, the torturer, the killer.

The playboy has a hard time finding himself in all of this. Adonism is not a too versatile field of endeavor after all. Innocence also has a small corner in it. Innocence is the stage where the phenomenon of life has yet to step into the world of anguish and vision. This brings in the grave question of how short-changed is the "permissive" youth of today if to be worthy of sex is to have passed the threshold of innocence into the craggy landscape of good and evil and the improbable grace to be sought in it.

This seems also to confirm that the esthetogenetic process is beyond innocence, beyond the green pastures of early youth, where anguish is but a flutter of the heart.

Civitate Dei is then a city of adults. Indeed, the city is by man that has grown into the full self, far past the innocence of the Garden of Eden, beyond the collages of perception, into the structure of understanding and the sufferance of its limitations. There, operating in an otherness that slowly converts itself into the inwardness of a new, larger creature, inclusive of the I and Thou, strands of joyfulness again begin to radiate outwardly and now from what has become the core of the city, the transhuman milieu of Civitate Dei.

| | | | | |
|---|---|---|---|---|
| Anguish − Joy | | = | Desperation | |
| Anguish + Joy | | = | Compassion | |
| Anguish + Joy + Lust | | = | Orgasm | |
| Anguish + Joy + Vision | | = | Creation | = Esthetogenesis |
| Mineral | No orgasm | = | No reproduction | |
| Vegetal | No orgasm | = | Reproduction | |
| Animal | Orgasm | = | Reproduction | |
| Human | Orgasm | = | Reproduction + Joy + Anguish | |
| Mental | "Orgasm" | = | Esthetogenesis | |

*As the end of a process, man is absurd. As the beginning of a process, man might be hopeless, desperate, but never absurd. We stand where the magnetic field is just beginning to orient each particle (monad). The total pattern is far off in the future but the magnet is operative and the particles will orient themselves. In reality the magnet (which stands as God) is itself self-constructing and the force field is not just undefined but also highly improbable, not absurd, just inconceivable.*

# CIVITATE DEI (The Mutant Man)

The complexity of the city acts upon man not only culturally but also genetically. The individuals more attuned to its complexity will be more consistently reproduced through the parental chain. The ones not so attuned will tend to leave per se or not have offspring. More important still is the nature of the intimate connection between the urbanite and the urbis. If it is love or hatred, convenience, opportunism, thirst for learning or for luxury, give and take or parasitism—if any of those powerful but "intangible" forces and stresses have any genetic moorings, then the species itself is directly dependent on what the urban atmosphere is, to develop, to evolve into persons more and more intensely marked by those genetic empathies favored by the milieu. For a self-responsible and passionate population, the milieu is constructive and hopeful and is worthy of reverence. A squalid milieu by converse will favor genetic selection of diminished vitality on the one hand and of harsh and belligerent natures on the other.

## URBAN MUTANT

Natural selection works herself in the quasi fictional natures of the city and fitness of ever changing kinds is going to make for the prevailing characters. The New Yorker is of a different breed from the Iowa farmer not only culturally but genetically, especially once the breeding has gotten its own momentum. If the New Yorker was one of a kind, and not one of many New York kinds, and greed was its kind, then the race would nurture in her New York womb a hominid possessed by a novel single-mindedness and empathy toward greediness.

How much of this applies to the "Western Culture," and how powerful the sway might be, is a grave question. If we concede also that greed has to feed upon itself once the peons and meek (the not fit) are weeded out, we are left with a self-destructing phenomenon, a nemesis hidden within the genetic enigma and brought to fruition by existential choices and inclinations marking the environment in such ways as to snowball the becoming into its own destruction.

If this takes place in the context of civilization, then the responsibility of the leading members of society takes also a new dimension. To the social and cultural pressures that can only work on the acquired character of the person so that his offspring can at least theoretically move to any of the social and cultural niches not touched by the parent is added the far more persistent, i.e. serious, pressure of slow or rapid mutation processes governed by the iron rule of "natural" selection where the "twist" is in the transformation and transformism of the natural by the doings of man.

Natural selection for the city dweller is mostly urban selection, as natural in this case refers to conditions which are of an urban nature and urbanization is still in progression, investing larger and larger populations.

## "FREE" ENTERPRISE MUTANT

The desolation of the ghetto at the end might not be the most damaging aspect of the city, nor the violent man moved to crime as he is poor in offspring. What will do man in is the increasing predominance of the socially and economically aggressive type motivated by patent or hidden greed as he is successful not just culturally but also genetically through the relatively larger spawning of offspring, who are often endowed by both parents with the genetic cunning favorable to the survival-plus of the competitive "free" enterprise society.

(Japan might be a phenomenon to watch closely for the possible detection of a breed of man frightfully fit for a society clad in steel and plastic and amiss of the emotion of the tender flesh.)

To foster the personal life of people sensitized by the broad spectrum of life is then sufficient only if we are able at the same time to put them in the position of breeding their own kind, at rates which are greater than the rates attributed to the greedy kind.

How the law of probability would give us promising statistics is still a guess but it would seem that the offspring of two white cats will be a white kitten more probably than if both parents were calicos. Notwithstanding quantitative vagueness, the environment—physical and non-physical—plays a determinate part in forging future man, and while the cultural aspects are shed at each life termination, the number and the nature of "selected" offspring is a branding that feeds its own kind more and more into the dominant mutation.

## TERRITORIALITY AND REVERENCE

If holding and controlling, the so-called "territorial imperative," means at a certain point aggression, then aggres-

## ASSUMPTIONS

*1. Consequent to the fortuitous or divine triggering of life, the universe of mass-energy is in the process of etherealizing itself into spirit.*

*2. Intrinsic to this metamorphosis of mass-energy into spirit is the ever-increasing complexity of systems carrying on the transformation.*

*3. The spatial mechanism of putting more into less allowing for the incrementation of complexity, is the miniaturization process.*

*4. On this earth, the most comprehensive structure embodying the becoming of etherealization is the city.*

## CONSEQUENCES

A. Thus the city, this etherealization "machine," is rigorously governed by the physical energetic rules of complexity-miniaturization.

B. Among the many options offered to contemporary man, the complex miniaturized city is the least optional inasmuch as it is mandatory for the spirit of the earth.

C. This city is a social, political, economic, moral, cultural imperative and under the demographic pressure it is also a survival necessity.

D. This gives the lie to most of our priorities and demythologizes practical man, as his paradigms are bankrupt. The real man is the man of the spirit.

THEREFORE, FOR REAL MAN, THE CITY IS THE CIVITATE DEI.

sion it is. We made it into the killer instinct quite unreasonably, as the killer instinct appears to be the way of last resort for even most of the so-called criminals. More relevant than the territorial imperative already disputed by some is that of the three kinds of respect man might show toward the environment—the coerced kind, the self-interest kind, the reverential kind—only this last has anything to offer of a hopeful nature. The other two are directly related to the greedy nature of aggressive men: in the first, the greed and power holding of minorities; in the second, the opulence syndrome of the affluent (democratic?) society.

As for survival, it is reasonable to assume that the kind of survival of the human species is of a different nature than the survival, let's say, of the scorpion species. If in the two or three million years the scorpion has not changed, then its aim must be the perpetuation of a certain circular event, a perpetual, self-repeating ritual of a combination of protein-enzymes, etc., the survival of a status quo. Can that be the kind of human survival or if that is the eventual kind for an arrested (fossil) human kind, is our time the time for its beginning? It would be a fantastic coincidence of time, space and our personal presence. Far more probable is that our present survival, as it has been for the last many millions of years is a survival of a progressive momentum: a progressive, evolutive survival. Then our genetic structure is still very much in turmoil. We are making ourselves genetically as a species while constructing ourselves culturally one by one in our individual cycles.

## THE CITY IN THE IMAGE OF MAN

The city of the compassionate man, the evolving man by definition if life is seen as the transformation of matter into spirit, the lovable city is the Civitate Dei if it is by its interceding that the mutant man is abundantly the man that does out of love. Furthermore, as the lovable city is not a withered and slumbering thing, it is also the city of "vision."

The lovable city is then the only city that has any promises for the species as well as being the only city that can offer personal fulfillment. If, furthermore, the city is the cradle of cultural and civilizing pressures as it seems to be said by history, then the desirability of the Civitate Dei becomes an imperative. The only path in the forest of the future that will conduct man into the light of grace.

Civitate Dei, the "Loving City," cannot ignore either one of the genetic and cultural markings. In a way the religious would tend to influence the genetic, in the sense that there is the field where a trend can become an "instinct" and man would become innately more compassionate, making himself into a more loving species. The secular would tend to the cultural, bringing more knowledge and creativity to man.

The resultant of the compassionate and the "visionary" would be the esthetogenesis of the extant world, the transbiological creation of reality resultant from the combined trust of genetic etherealization (love, theological) and cultural metamorphosis (knowledge, ontological).

Is there any difference between the aim of the city and the aim of the Catholic (universal) Church? They are one and the same. In a very physical way, the city is the Church, a place for reverence because it is the place where the highest event of this earth, man, is battling the wages of fear, ignorance, deception, hatred, despair and sloth.

Is there a contradiction, and where is it, between the stern character of the survival of the fittest, picturing the winning animal as the stronger, most cunning, but not by a long shot most lovable, and the mutant most apt to live in and foster the Civitate Dei?

From the economical standpoint man might have to bow to homo sapiens and homo creator and keep homo economicus in its instrumental, supportive position.

Politically man might have to calibrate the one-man one-vote so as to achieve the only true democratic society where authority is totally separated from power, and power is acting under the guidance of the knowledge authority is based on. (Authority as convincing power not as coercive power.)

Morally, we might have to reach a clear understanding of the difference between piousness and compassion and why one might contradict the other.

Ontologically, we better take sides in the struggle between what fosters the life of the spirit and what does not, as one is moving with the esthetogenesis of the real while the other is obscurantism.

## TRANSFIGURATION

At all levels, the lever for survival and fitness is not acquiescence but intensity and commitment, and survival-fitness has to count not on conservation (scorpion) but transfiguration (man-spirit). Furthermore, to go wrong in any of those is to defile the mutant which can etherealize the physical universe. It is not to achieve Civitate Dei. To go right is in any case a quasi-endless journey into the future once such future is at least suggested by the obscure gropings of biogenesis and by the first unsure steps of homogenesis.

*Earlier versions of the chapters in this volume were written during the years noted below.*

The Sculpture Earth (1961)
Craftsman and Obsolescence (1963 and 1966)
New Environment (1965)
Bulldozer Man (1966)
Topics (1968)
Man and Separateness (1968)
The Poor Country (1968)
A View of the United States—Looking Toward the Bicentennial of 1976 (1969)
Back to Nature? (1969)
Going to Nowhere, Anyone? (1969)
Simulation and Becoming (1970)
Estheticism and Esthetogenesis (1970)
The Inner and the Outer in Arid Land (1970)
Quiet Greed (1970)
Flight from Flatness (1970)
Thirteen Questions on Arcology (1971)
Function Follows Form (1971)
Transarcology (1971)
Psychosomatic Man (1971)
Utopia (Practical Man, Real Man) (1971)
Arcomedia (1971)
The American Withdrawal from America (1969)
Joy and Anguish in the Lust Bag (1971)
Civitate Dei (1971)
A Canadian Alternative? (1971)
The Beautiful Body Is an Awesome Powerhouse (1972)
Pollution as Entropy (1972)